get crocked.

Slow Cooker
Soups &
Stews

Contents

117

178

242

Fisherman's Cioppino Stew 214

There is nothing like coming home on a cool day to the warmth and comfort of a big bowl of soup or a hearty helping of stew. And you know what's even better? Having dinner already finished when you walk in the door! There are many reasons why I love making soups and stews in the slow cooker—not only does the delicious aroma of dinner fill the air, but you also know you'll be able to relax and enjoy a great dish with little to no clean up. In *Get Crocked Slow Cooker Soups & Stews*, I am happy to share some of my favorite (and simple!) recipes, from timeless classics like Chicken Noodle Soup to soon-to-be favorites like Barbecue Beef Stew. Regardless of your tastes, you're sure to find recipes to keep—and share—for a lifetime. Enjoy!

Happy Crocking!

xOxO, Jenn Bare

Slow Cooker
101

Few meals are as easy and delicious as slow-cooked soups and stews, but it's best to know the basics before you begin. With these simple tips and tricks, you'll be a slow cooker master in no time!

1. Size Things Up

Make sure your slow cooker is the appropriate size. A family of two to three should use a 4-quart slow cooker for regular meals and a 6-quart slow cooker for big pots of soup or stew. A model that's too big can cause food to cook too quickly or burn. For best results, make sure your slow cooker is ½ to ⅔ of the way full. Underfilling the slow cooker can dry out your meal.

2. Learn to Layer

Sure, you can just toss all your ingredients into the slow cooker—but placing them in a certain order often makes for better texture in the final product. Root vegetables, such as carrots and potatoes, take longer to cook than meat, for instance, so you should place them on the bottom of the slow cooker. And while you're at it, chop ingredients in a uniform size; it's another step that helps ensure everything cooks evenly.

3. Make Good Timing

Use a programmable slow cooker to let meals cook all day while you're gone. It will automatically switch to WARM when the timer goes off. Keep in mind that you want to save some ingredients for last, though. Dairy products, such as sour cream and cream cheese, can break down if left cooking for hours, so add them during the last 15 to 30 minutes of cooking (unless otherwise specified). The same rules apply when it comes to breakfast. If your recipe calls for eggs, dairy or meat (ingredients that can be overcooked), prep the meal in a slow cooker liner or large bowl before you go to sleep, then set your alarm according to the cook time. When you wake up, all you'll have to do is add the liner to the slow cooker and turn it on before you go back to bed for a few more hours. Another food that's easy to overcook: pasta. Only add noodles during the last hour of cooking to keep them from turning to mush. You can also precook pasta until it's al dente and add it to the slow cooker during the last 15 minutes of cooking.

4. Practice Patience

Resist the urge to take a peek while your food's still simmering. If you lift the lid, moisture and heat can escape, causing the dish to dry out and take longer to cook. So always keep the lid on your slow cooker when it's in use (unless otherwise specified).

5. Add Finishing Touches

If you want to make your meal even more mouth-watering, stick it in the oven to brown up a bit before serving. Many slow cooker inserts, but not lids, are oven-safe (Word to the wise: Make sure you use potholders—the stoneware will be hot!).

The Classics

Once you master these tasty and timeless standards, your family will be refilling bowl after bowl!

Serve this to warm up the family—you'll be the hero of your home!

Chicken Broth

YIELD 12 bowls **I COOK TIME** 4 to 8 hours

Ingredients

4	bone-in chicken breasts and/or thighs
1	onion, quartered
1	c. carrots, diced
2	celery stalks
2	cloves garlic
2–3	sprigs thyme
2–3	sprigs rosemary
3	bay leaves
15	whole peppercorns
1–2	T. kosher salt

Directions

1. Place all ingredients into slow cooker and cover with water.
2. Cover and cook on HIGH for 4 hours or LOW for 8 hours.
3. Strain liquid over large pitcher or bowl. Discard vegetables, peppercorns and herbs. If desired, you can save cooked chicken to use for other dishes.
4. Store chicken broth in mason jars and refrigerate up to 2 days or freeze for several months. Fat that rises to top of storing jar or container can be removed easily after chilling.

Better Than Basic

When you have a high-quality, homemade chicken broth on hand for soups, there's just no comparison. Buying canned broth is fine for saving time, but putting the effort (and all the flavor!) into making your own will give you so much pride when you make a truly homemade meal!

Broccoli Three Cheese Soup

YIELD 6 bowls **I COOK TIME** 6 hours 15 minutes

Ingredients

- 2 T. butter
- 2 T. flour
- 2 c. milk
- 1 (32-oz.) container chicken stock
- 1 small yellow onion, minced
- 3 c. fresh broccoli, chopped
- ½ t. salt
- 1 t. pepper
- ½ t. ground nutmeg
- 1 c. shredded sharp cheddar cheese
- 1 c. shredded Gruyère cheese
- 1 c. shredded Monterey Jack cheese

Directions

1. Place a large skillet over medium-low heat and add butter. Once butter has melted, slowly sprinkle in flour and whisk. Continue adding flour until a thick yellow paste forms. Whisk in the milk, followed by chicken stock.
2. Place minced onion in slow cooker. Pour in liquid from the skillet. Stir in broccoli, salt and pepper.
3. Cover and cook on LOW for 6 hours, or until the onion is completely softened.
4. Remove lid and add nutmeg. Stir in all three cheeses.
5. Cover and cook on LOW for 15 minutes, or until cheeses are melted.

If you have some extra bread on hand, toast it and crumble your own croutons!

You can also add noodles in the last 20 minutes of cooking.

Easy
Matzo Ball Soup

YIELD 6 to 8 bowls | **COOK TIME** 8 hours 20 minutes

Ingredients

2   large carrots, peeled and sliced

2   stalks celery, chopped

1   medium yellow onion, diced

4   boneless, skinless chicken breasts

2   t. minced garlic

1   bay leaf

4   c. water

4   c. chicken stock

1   t. salt

½   t. pepper

½   c. matzo ball mix

1   t. dried thyme

Directions

1. Place carrots, celery and onion on the bottom of slow cooker. Add chicken breast and cover with garlic, bay leaf, water, stock, salt and pepper.

2. Cover and cook on LOW for 8 hours.

3. While soup is cooking, prepare matzo balls according to package directions. Cover and refrigerate for 15 minutes. Shape chilled dough into 1-in. balls.

4. After 8 hours, remove chicken and shred with two forks. Return chicken to the slow cooker.

5. Place matzo balls into the soup.

6. Cover and cook on LOW for an additional 20 minutes.

Chicken Noodle Soup

YIELD 6 to 8 bowls **I COOK TIME** 8 hours 20 minutes

Ingredients

- 8 c. chicken broth
- 3 large carrots, peeled and cut into ¼-in. chunks
- 2 stalks celery, peeled and cut into ¼-in. chunks
- 1 medium yellow onion, chopped
- 2 cloves garlic, minced
- 1 bay leaf
- ½ t. dried thyme
  Salt and pepper, to taste
- 4 boneless, skinless chicken breasts
- 3 c. wide egg noodles, uncooked

Directions

1. Combine broth, carrots, celery, onion, garlic, bay leaf, thyme, salt, pepper and chicken in slow cooker.
2. Cover and cook on LOW for 8 hours.
3. Remove chicken and shred using two forks. Discard bay leaf. Add noodles to the slow cooker and cook for an additional 20 minutes. Return shredded chicken to the soup and mix well.
4. Serve alone or with saltine crackers.

Classic Comfort

Out of all the soups I've ever had, chicken noodle soup is still one of my all-time favorites! Many people associate this soup with being home sick because its classic taste is just so comforting. But not only does it warm you up when you have a cold, but it can also help clear your nasal passages!

French Onion Soup

YIELD 8 to 10 bowls | **COOK TIME** 4 hours or 6 to 7 hours

Ingredients

2	T. unsalted butter
3	large yellow onions, sliced
1	c. dry white or red wine
1	(32-oz.) container beef broth
1	t. Worcestershire sauce
½	t. salt
½	t. thyme
1	t. minced garlic
1	bay leaf
8–10	slices toasted French bread
1	c. shredded Gruyère cheese

It never hurts to have extra bread on the side for this soup!

Directions

1. Heat a large skillet over medium and add butter. When butter melts, add onions. Increase heat to medium-high and cook for 10 minutes. Add wine.
2. Pour skillet mixture into slow cooker. Add remaining ingredients (excluding bread and Gruyère cheese).
3. Cover and cook on HIGH for 4 hours or on LOW for 6 to 7 hours.
4. Dish soup in oven-safe serving bowls and place a piece of toasted French bread in each. Top with shredded Gruyère cheese.
5. Place bowls on a baking sheet, then broil for 2 minutes, or until cheese bubbles.

Italian Wedding Soup

YIELD 8 bowls **I** **COOK TIME** 7 hours 30 minutes

Ingredients

MEATBALLS

- 2 T. olive oil
- 1 lb. lean ground beef
- ½ lb. sweet Italian sausage
- 1 egg, beaten
- ¼ c. Italian bread crumbs
- 2 T. Italian seasoning
- 1 t. minced garlic
- ½ t. pepper
- ½ t. salt
- ¼ c. Parmesan cheese

SOUP

- 1 medium yellow onion, minced
- 2 large carrots, minced
- 2 stalks celery, finely chopped
- 2 boneless, skinless chicken breasts
- 6 c. chicken stock
- 1 bay leaf
- 1 ½ t. garlic powder
- ¼ t. pepper
- ½ c. cavatelli pasta, cooked
- 2 c. baby spinach
- ¼ c. Parmesan cheese, to garnish

Directions

MEATBALLS

1. Combine ingredients and form into ¾-inch meatballs, yielding a total of about 5 dozen.
2. Add meatballs to a large greased skillet and heat over medium-high until brown on all sides.
3. Place meatballs on a paper towel-lined plate while preparing the soup.

SOUP

1. Place onion, carrots and celery into slow cooker. Add meatballs, chicken breast, chicken stock, bay leaf, garlic powder and pepper.
2. Cover and cook on LOW for 7 hours.
3. Discard bay leaf and remove chicken breasts to shred. Return shredded chicken to the slow cooker and cover. Stir in pasta and spinach.
4. Serve garnished with Parmesan cheese, if desired.

If you love garlic, add fresh cloves to your soup.

Loaded
Baked Potato Soup

YIELD 6 bowls **I COOK TIME** 4 hours 20 minutes to 8 hours 20 minutes

Ingredients

- 6 large russet potatoes, washed, peeled and diced
- 1 large yellow onion, chopped
- 1 (32-oz.) container chicken broth
- 3 t. minced garlic
- 3 T. unsalted butter
- 1 t. salt
- ½ t. pepper
- 1 c. milk
- 1 c. shredded sharp cheddar cheese
- 3 T. chopped green onions
- ½ (8-oz.) pkg. cream cheese
- 4 slices bacon, cooked and crumbled
- ½ c. shredded cheddar cheese, to garnish

Directions

1. Layer potatoes and onions in slow cooker. Add chicken broth, garlic, butter, salt and pepper.
2. Cover and cook on HIGH for 4 hours, on LOW for 6 hours or until potatoes are tender.
3. Press soup with a masher until the potatoes are coarsely chopped and the soup is slightly thickened.
4. Stir in milk, cheddar cheese, green onions and cream cheese.
5. Cover and cook for 20 minutes on LOW, or until cheeses are melted.
6. Garnish with bacon and cheese and serve.

Manhattan Clam Chowder

YIELD 8 bowls **I** **COOK TIME** 6 to 8 hours

Ingredients

- 1 (16-oz.) can clams, with liquid
- 1 (14.5 oz.) can fire roasted diced tomatoes
- 2 c. water
- 4 c. vegetable or chicken broth
- 2 c. split peas, sorted and double rinsed
- 2 stalks celery, chopped
- 2 large carrots, peeled and chopped
- 1 medium yellow onion, diced
- ¼ t. thyme
- 1 dash red pepper
- 1 bay leaf
- 1 t. salt
- ½ t. pepper

Directions

1. Drain claims and reserve liquid; cover and refrigerate. Add liquid to slow cooker.
2. Add all remaining ingredients except clams to slow cooker, cover and cook on LOW for 6 to 8 hours, or until vegetables and split peas are tender.
3. Stir in clams, cover and cook for an additional 30 minutes on LOW.
4. Discard bay leaf. If desired, lightly mash vegetables to thicken stew before serving.

Spicing It Up

There's nothing wrong with adding your own twist to a recipe, even if it's a classic like this one! This soup is also great with hot sauce for those who like things a little spicy. Simply add a few splashes of your favorite hot sauce when the soup finishes cooking, or just put it out as an option for guests.

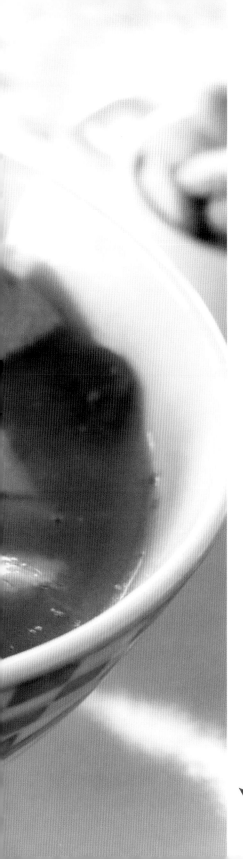

Chicken Kluski Soup

YIELD 6 to 8 bowls **I** **COOK TIME** 6 hours 30 minutes

Ingredients

SOUP

- 1 lb. boneless, skinless chicken breasts
- 1 medium yellow onion, chopped
- 2 garlic cloves, minced
- 2 carrots, peeled and chopped
- 2 stalks celery, chopped
- 1 bay leaf
- 1 (32-oz.) container chicken broth
- 1 c. water
- 1 t. pepper
- ½ t. salt
- 2 sprigs fresh thyme
- 2 T. minced fresh parsley
- 1 T. fresh basil

KLUSKI NOODLES

- 4 eggs
- 1 c. warm water
- 3 ⅓ c. flour
- 2 T. melted salted butter

Craving creamier soup? Add a can of cream of chicken just before serving.

Directions

1. Combine all soup ingredients except thyme, parsley and fresh basil in slow cooker.
2. Cover and cook on LOW for 6 hours.
3. Place fresh basil in slow cooker and stir. Cover and continue cooking while preparing kluski.
4. To make kluski, whisk eggs and water together in a medium bowl. Slowly add sifted flour while stirring with a fork; drizzle in butter and continue stirring.
5. To prepare kluski, either form into crescent shapes by hand then drop into slow cooker or drop batter, one spoonful at a time, into soup.
6. Cover and cook on LOW for 30 minutes or until kluski are cooked to your liking.
7. Remove bay leaf and discard. Just before serving, remove chicken breasts, shred or cut into bite-sized pieces and return to slow cooker.

Mushroom Barley Soup

YIELD 6 to 8 bowls **I COOK TIME** 4 to 6 hours

Ingredients

9 c. chicken broth
1 lb. fresh mushrooms, sliced
1 onion, diced
2 carrots, peeled and chopped
2 celery stalks, chopped
½ c. pearled barley
½ oz. dried porcini mushrooms
3 garlic cloves, minced
1 t. salt
½ t. dried thyme
½ t. pepper

Directions

1. Combine all ingredients in slow cooker.
2. Cover and cook on LOW for 4 to 6 hours.
3. Serve with a French baguette and a drizzle of truffle oil, if desired.

 # Red Beans and Rice

For a little extra protein, add 1 lb. Kielbasa sausage to this dish.

YIELD 6 bowls **I COOK TIME** 5 to 6 hours

Ingredients

- 1 medium yellow onion, diced
- 1 stalk celery, finely chopped
- ¾ t. pepper
- ½ t. salt
- 1 t. ground cumin
- 1 t. chili powder
- ½ t. smoked paprika
- 1 (30-oz.) can red beans, rinsed and drained
- ¾ c. rice
- 6 c. vegetable broth
- 3 green onions, chopped
- 1 medium tomato, diced

Directions

1. Place onions, celery and seasonings in a slow cooker.
2. Mash half of the beans and add them in the slow cooker. Pour the remaining unmashed beans on top. Add rice, broth, green onions and tomatoes.
3. Cover and cook on LOW for 5 to 6 hours, or until the rice is tender.

Split Pea Soup

YIELD 8 bowls **I** **COOK TIME** 6 to 8 hours

Ingredients

2	c. water
4	c. vegetable or chicken broth
2	c. split peas, sorted and double rinsed
2	stalks celery, chopped
2	large carrots, peeled and chopped
1	medium yellow onion, diced
¼	t. thyme
1	dash red pepper
1	bay leaf
1	t. salt
½	t. pepper
1	t. smoked paprika

Directions

1. Combine all ingredients in slow cooker.
2. Cover and cook on LOW for 6 to 8 hours, or until vegetables and split peas are tender.
3. Discard bay leaf. Press finished soup through a fine sieve and reheat to boiling point or smooth with a hand blender.

Tastier Texture

Sometimes when I make soup, I find that even the most delicious ingredients still lack a little something—texture! If you want your split pea soup to have a little more texture, try serving it garnished with some seasoned croutons. That little bit of crunch can really go a long way!

Split Pea with Ham

YIELD 8 bowls **I COOK TIME** 5 hours or 7 to 8 hours

Ingredients

3	c. split peas, washed and drained
4	c. chicken or vegetable broth
4	c. water
2	c. diced yellow onion
1	c. diced carrot
½	c. diced celery
8	oz. ham, trimmed of fat and diced
1	T. minced ginger
1	t. dried marjoram
1	potato, cut into small pieces
	Pepper, to taste
	Cooked and crumbled bacon, to garnish

Directions

1. Place peas in slow cooker. Add broth, water, onion, carrot, celery, ham, ginger, marjoram and potatoes. Stir to combine.
2. Cover and cook on LOW for 7 to 8 hours, or HIGH for 5 hours. Season with pepper and top with bacon, if desired.

Love leftovers?
This recipe can
be doubled very
easily!

Tomato-Basil Parmesan Soup

YIELD 8 bowls **I** **COOK TIME** 6 to 7 hours

Ingredients

- 1 (28-oz.) can crushed tomatoes
- ½ c. finely diced celery
- ½ c. finely diced carrots
- 1 medium yellow onion, minced
- 1 t. minced garlic
- 1 t. oregano
- 1 T. dried basil
- 1 T. fresh basil
- 4 c. chicken stock
- 1 bay leaf
- ½ c. butter
- ½ c. flour
- 1 c. Parmesan cheese, plus more to garnish
- 2 c. half-and-half
- 1 t. salt
- ¼ t. pepper
- 5 fresh basil leaves, chopped

Directions

1. Add tomatoes, celery, carrots, onion, garlic, oregano, dried basil, chicken stock and bay leaf in slow cooker.
2. Cover and cook on LOW for 6 to 7 hours.
3. Discard bay leaf. Heat a large skillet over medium-low heat and melt butter. Add flour and whisk for 3 to 4 minutes, or until a thick, off-white paste forms.
4. Slowly pour in 1 c. of soup from the slow cooker and whisk until smooth. Pour the contents of the skillet into the slow cooker. Stir in Parmesan cheese and half-and-half. Add salt, pepper and fresh basil.
5. Cover on WARM until ready to serve, making sure the soup does not boil. Top with Parmesan, if desired.

For a winning combination, serve with a toasted sandwich!

Vegetable Beef Soup

YIELD 10 bowls I **COOK TIME** 6 to 7 hours

Ingredients

1	lb. top sirloin, cut into cubes
1	medium yellow onion, diced
3	stalks celery, chopped
2	large potatoes, peeled and cubed
4	large carrots, peeled and chopped
1	(28-oz.) can diced tomatoes
1	(28-oz.) container beef broth
4	c. water
2	t. garlic powder
	Salt and pepper, to taste
2	bay leaves
2 ½	c. assorted frozen vegetables

Directions

1. Place beef, onion, celery, potatoes and carrots in slow cooker. Add diced tomatoes, beef broth, water, seasoning and bay leaves in soup.
2. Cover and cook on HIGH for 5 to 6 hours.
3. Add frozen vegetables. Cover and cook on HIGH for 1 hour, or until vegetables are soft.

Before adding it to your soup, brown seasoned meat with 1 T. oil in a skillet over medium heat to lock in flavor.

 # Corn and Red Pepper Chowder

YIELD 5 bowls **I COOK TIME** 4 hours 30 minutes to 6 hours 30 minutes

Ingredients

- 2 T. olive oil
- 1 medium yellow onion, diced
- 2 garlic cloves, minced
- 1 medium red bell pepper, seeded and diced, plus more to garnish
- 3 medium potatoes, diced (about 1 lb.)
- 4 c. frozen sweet corn kernels, divided (approx. 4 ears fresh corn), plus more to garnish
- 4 c. vegetable broth
- 1 t. ground cumin
- ½ t. smoked paprika
- ⅛ t. cayenne pepper
- 1 t. kosher salt
- 1 c. milk or half-and-half

  Salt and pepper, to taste

  Sliced green onions and sour cream, to garnish

  Cheese of your choice, to garnish

Directions

1. Place olive oil in a pan over medium heat. Sauté onion and garlic, stirring occasionally, until transparent and soft—about 5 minutes. Do not burn!
2. Mix onion in slow cooker with red bell pepper, potatoes, 1 c. corn, broth, cumin, smoked paprika, cayenne pepper and kosher salt.
3. Cover and cook on HIGH for 4 to 6 hours, until potatoes are tender.
4. Turn off slow cooker and remove lid. With a hand blender, puree soup.
5. Ladle one cup of soup into a bowl and stir in milk or half-and-half to combine, then return to slow cooker. Turn slow cooker back on and stir in remaining corn.
6. Cover and cook on LOW for another 30 minutes.
7. Season with salt and pepper to taste. Serve topped with additional garnishes.

Garnish with parsley for an extra pop of color.

Paleo Fire-Roasted Tomato Soup

YIELD 10 bowls **I COOK TIME** 3 to 4 hours or 6 to 7 hours

Ingredients

4	T. coconut oil
2	medium yellow onions, thinly sliced
1–2	t. sea salt
3	t. curry powder
1	t. ground coriander
1	t. ground cumin
½	t. red pepper flakes
2	(28-oz.) cans fire-roasted whole tomatoes
5	c. water
1	(14-oz.) can coconut milk
	Basil leaf, to garnish

If you desire thinner soup, replace coconut oil with water.

Directions

1. Melt coconut oil in large saucepan over medium-high heat. Add onions and sauté until tender, but not browned.
2. Add all seasonings and spices and sauté for another minute.
3. Transfer cooked onions and spices to slow cooker.
4. Add tomatoes and 5 c. of water to slow cooker.
5. Cover and cook on HIGH for 3 hours or on LOW for 6 hours.
6. Puree soup with a hand blender, or add contents to a stand blender and blend until smooth. Add contents back to slow cooker, add coconut milk and stir.
7. Cover and cook for 1 hour on LOW. Top with basil leaf, if desired.

Pumpkin Bisque

YIELD 4 bowls **I COOK TIME** 4 hours 15 minutes to 5 hours

Ingredients

1 (30-oz.) can pumpkin pie mixture
1 (15-oz.) can pumpkin
1 (28-oz.) can chicken broth
½ c. water
½ t. salt
¼ t. white pepper
¾ t. ground ginger
1 c. half-and-half
Sour cream, to garnish
Parsley, to garnish

Directions

1. In slow cooker, combine all ingredients except half-and-half and sour cream (if using).
2. Cover and cook on LOW for 4 to 5 hours.
3. Stir in half-and-half.
4. Cover and cook an additional 15 minutes.
5. Serve garnished with sour cream and parsley, if desired.

Fall Favorite

Everyone loves anything and everything pumpkin when the leaves start to change, whether it be pumpkin pie, pumpkin-spiced lattes or even just a handful of pumpkin seeds. I love this pumpkin bisque because of its versatility. Serve it as a starter or have it on its own for a light lunch!

Chicken and Black Bean Soup

YIELD 4 bowls **I COOK TIME** 3 to 4 hours

Ingredients

4   chicken breasts or thighs, boneless, skin removed

1   medium onion, finely chopped

1   (10-oz.) can tomatoes, diced with green chilies

1   (14-oz.) can chicken broth

1   (15-oz.) can black beans

1   c. frozen corn

4   oz. chopped green chilies

2   t. cumin

1   T. chili powder

1   t. salt

    Sliced avocado, shredded cheese, sour cream, fresh cilantro and/or fried tortilla strips, to garnish

Directions

1. Add all ingredients except garnishes to slow cooker.
2. Cover and cook on HIGH for 3 to 4 hours, or until chicken is cooked.
3. Remove chicken from soup with a slotted spoon to leave juices in slow cooker.
4. Carefully remove chicken from slow cooker and shred or chop. Return to slow cooker and stir well.
5. Top with sliced avocado, shredded cheese, sour cream, fresh cilantro and/or fried tortilla strips.

Add green and red peppers for fuller flavor and more color.

Best-Ever Beef Stew

YIELD 6 bowls **I COOK TIME** 4 to 5 hours or 8 to 9 hours

Ingredients

- 1 lb. stewing beef
- 1 large onion,
  halved and thinly sliced
- 2 medium carrots,
  peeled and thinly sliced
- 2 large potatoes,
  cut into small chunks
- 1–1 ½ c. rutabaga,
  peeled and diced
- 1 c. green beans,
  cut into small pieces
- 1 bay leaf
- ½ t. dried thyme
- 1 packet onion soup mix
- 1 garlic clove, crushed
- 3 c. beef stock
- 2 T. light brown sugar
- ¾ t. salt
- 2 t. Worcestershire sauce
  Pepper, to taste
- 3 T. all-purpose flour
- 2 t. tomato paste

*Rutabaga can
be omitted,
if desired.
To substitute,
increase potatoes
and carrots.*

Directions

1. In a skillet with olive oil, brown stewing beef.
2. Combine everything except flour and tomato paste in slow cooker and stir to combine.
3. Cover and cook on LOW for 8 to 9 hours or on HIGH for 4 to 5 hours, until beef is tender and potatoes are fork tender.
4. Stir stew once or twice as it cooks, if possible.
5. About 30 minutes before serving, transfer a ladle of the broth to a small mixing bowl.
6. Add flour and tomato paste and whisk until smooth. Stir mixture into stew and cook for remaining half hour.

 German Goulash

YIELD 6 to 8 bowls **I COOK TIME** 4 to 5 hours or 6 to 7 hours

Ingredients

1 (14.5-oz.) can whole peeled tomatoes

1 T. tomato paste

4 potatoes, peeled and diced

2 lb. beef, stewing lean meat, trimmed and cubed

2 large carrots, peeled and diced

2 large onions, peeled and diced

1 T. parsley

2 T. smoked paprika

1 T. garlic powder

½ T. thyme

1 c. dry red wine

Salt and pepper, to taste

Sour cream and German noodles, to garnish

Directions

1. To make tomato sauce, mix peeled tomatoes and tomato paste in a blender until smooth.

2. Place potatoes in slow cooker, then cover with beef, carrots, onion and tomato sauce.

3. Top with herbs and spices.

4. Pour in wine.

5. Cover and cook on LOW for 6 to 7 hours or on HIGH for 4 to 5 hours.

6. Serve with sour cream and German noodles.

Chili Cook-Off

Once you master these hot, amazing meals in a bowl, you'll be wishing winter would last all year long!

A little extra color on top goes a long way!

Black Bean Turkey Chili

YIELD 8 bowls **I COOK TIME** 8 hours

Ingredients

½ onion, diced
2 carrots, chopped
2 celery stalks, chopped
1 lb. ground turkey breast
1 T. olive oil
1 (14-oz.) can black beans, undrained
1 (14-oz.) can diced tomatoes
1 ½ c. beef broth
1 (6-oz.) can tomato paste
1 (4-oz.) can diced green or red chilies
1 ½ T. chili powder
1 t. cumin
1 T. minced garlic
1 bay leaf

Directions

1. Place onion, carrot and celery in the bottom of slow cooker.
2. Add raw ground turkey, in chunks.
3. Add remaining ingredients.
4. Cover and cook on LOW for 8 hours, stirring and breaking up meat after 4 hours.
5. Remove bay leaf before serving.

Crowd-Pleaser

This chili is a great choice when you need a healthy and delicious meal. Plus, it's an easy crowd-pleaser. It's mild enough for the kiddos to eat and it's definitely delicious enough to please even the pickiest adult. And if you feel like adding a twist, add frozen corn or diced sweet potatoes.

Denver
Bison Chili

YIELD 8 to 10 bowls **I** **COOK TIME** 6 to 7 hours

Ingredients

- 2 lb. ground bison
  Salt and pepper, to taste
- 1 onion, chopped
- 2 t. minced garlic
- 2 t. ground cumin
- ¾ t. cayenne pepper
- 1–2 T. chili powder
- 1 poblano pepper,
  seeded and chopped
- 2 (14 ½-oz.) cans diced
  tomatoes
- 1 (8-oz.) can diced green chilies
- 2 (15-oz.) cans chili beans
- 2 (14 ½-oz.) cans kidney beans,
  undrained

Directions

1. Crumble raw bison into
   slow cooker.
2. Sprinkle meat with salt
   and pepper.
3. Place onions over top meat,
   followed by remaining
   seasonings and poblano pepper.
4. Add tomatoes, green chilies,
   chili beans and kidney beans.
5. Cover and cook on LOW for 6
   to 7 hours.
6. Break up cooked meat with
   a wooden spoon and stir to
   incorporate into chili.
7. Taste and add additional
   seasonings as needed.

Turkey Three-Bean Chili

You can also add about ½ c. chicken broth from a leftover meal, if desired.

YIELD 8 bowls **I** **COOK TIME** 2 hours 30 minutes to 3 hours or 4 to 5 hours

Ingredients

1 lb. ground turkey

1 small onion, chopped

1 red bell pepper, chopped

1 green pepper, chopped

2 celery stalks, chopped

1 (16-oz.) can pinto beans, drained

1 (15-oz.) can dark red kidney beans, drained

1 (15-oz.) can black beans, drained

2 (14 ½-oz) cans tomatoes, diced

1 (8-oz.) can tomato sauce

1 (4-oz.) can green chilies, chopped

2 cloves garlic, peeled and crushed

3 T. chili powder

1 t. pepper

1 t. ground cumin

¼ t. cayenne pepper

Salt, to taste

Shredded cheese of your choice, to garnish

Sour cream, to garnish

Directions

1. Brown ground turkey in a skillet with onion, bell pepper and celery.
2. Halfway through browning turkey, drain liquid from the bottom to help it brown.
3. Transfer to slow cooker and add all remaining ingredients.
4. Cover and cook on LOW for 4 to 5 hours or on HIGH for 2 hours 30 minutes to 3 hours.
5. Serve with shredded cheese and a dollop of sour cream.

15-Bean Chicken Chili

YIELD 8 bowls **I** **COOK TIME** 8 hours

Ingredients

1 ½ c. dried 15-bean soup

1 lb. boneless, skinless chicken breast, uncooked and cubed

¼ c. finely chopped onion

3 garlic cloves, minced

1 (16-oz.) can tomatillos, drained and chopped

1 (14 ½-oz.) can diced tomatoes with green chilies

2 c. chicken broth

1 (4-oz.) can diced green chilies, undrained

½ t. dried oregano

½ t. crushed coriander seeds

¼ t. ground cumin

3 T. lime juice

Salt and pepper, to taste

Sharp cheddar cheese, shredded, to garnish

Directions

1. Place beans in a bowl and cover with water to soak overnight.
2. Next day: Drain beans and add to slow cooker.
3. Place all remaining ingredients except cheese in slow cooker.
4. Cover and cook on LOW for 8 hours.

Serve with fresh bread for delicious dipping!

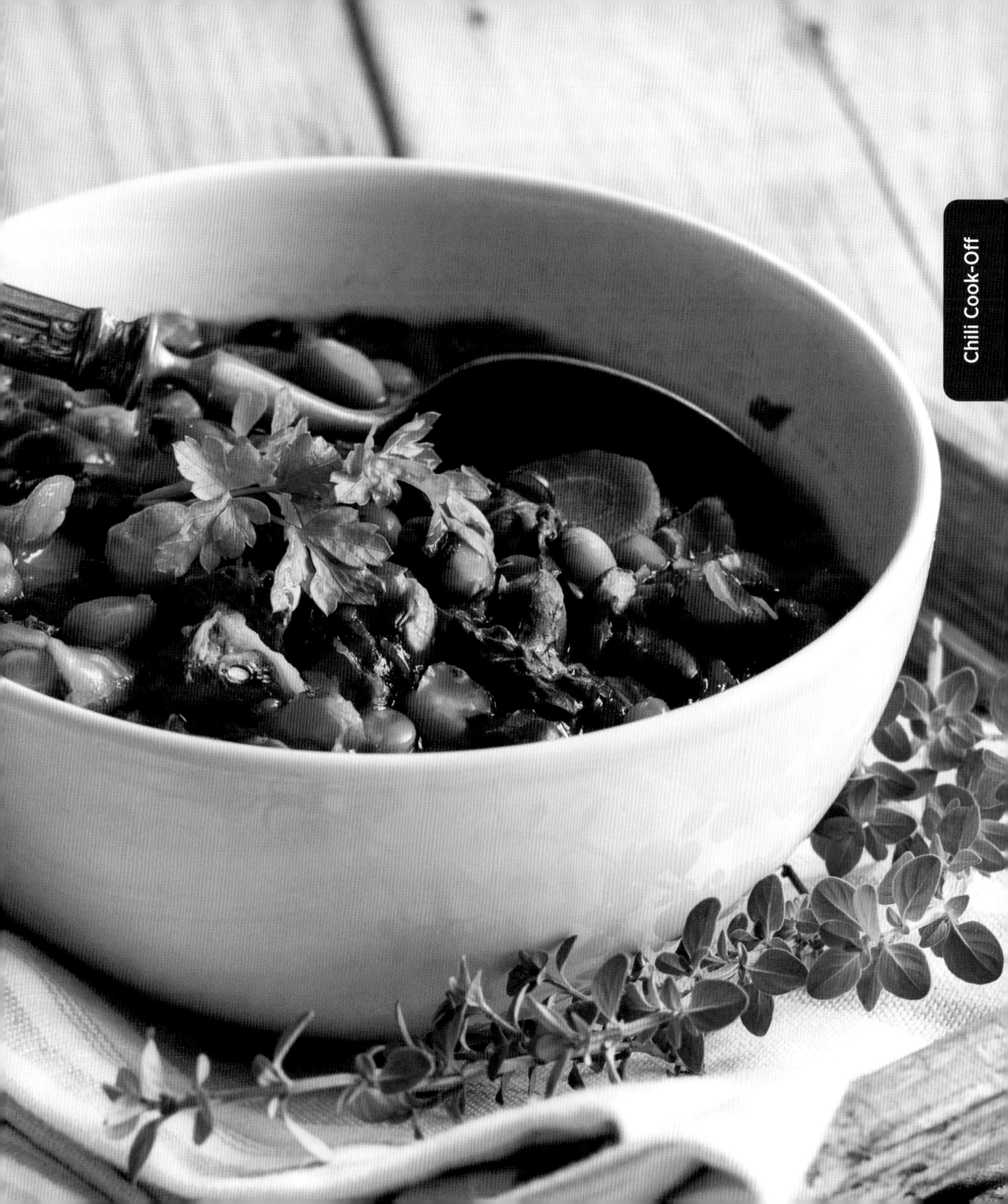

Pumpkin Pinto Chili

YIELD 12 servings **I** **COOK TIME** 6 hours 30 minutes to 9 hours 30 minutes

Ingredients

- 1 pkg. pinto beans, rinsed and sorted
- 1 smoked ham hock
- 1 large onion, diced
- 8 c. chicken broth
- 1 (7-oz.) can chipotles in adobo sauce
- 1 (15-oz.) can pure pumpkin
- 2 T. chili powder
- 1 t. allspice

Directions

1. Pour beans into slow cooker. Add ham hock, diced onion and chicken stock.
2. Strain adobo sauce from can of chipotles and add sauce into slow cooker.
3. Chop desired amount of chipotles and add to slow cooker.
4. Cover and cook on LOW for 8 to 9 hours or on HIGH for 6 hours.
5. After beans are tender, remove bone from ham hock and add ham back into slow cooker.
6. Stir in pumpkin, chili powder and allspice. Cook on LOW for an additional 30 minutes, then keep warm until ready to serve.

Top with shredded cheese of your choice!

 # Classic Vegetarian Chili

YIELD 12 bowls **I COOK TIME** 6 hours

Ingredients

- 1 onion, chopped
- 1 green bell pepper, chopped
- 2 zucchini, chopped
- 2 celery stalks, chopped
- 1 (11-oz.) can condensed black bean soup
- 1 (15-oz.) can kidney beans, drained and rinsed
- 1 (15-oz.) can garbanzo beans, drained and rinsed
- 1 (16-oz.) can hot chili beans
- 1 (29-oz.) can tomatoes, crushed, or 1 (14 ½-oz.) can tomato puree
- 1 (15-oz.) can whole kernel corn, drained
- 1–2 jalapeños, chopped
- 1 (4-oz.) can diced green chilies
- 2 garlic cloves, chopped
- 1 T. chili powder
- 2 t. cumin
- 1 T. dried parsley
- 1 T. dried oregano
- 1 T. dried basil
- 1 T. cilantro

Directions

1. Sauté onion, bell pepper, zucchini and celery in a skillet for 4 to 5 minutes.
2. Combine black beans, kidney beans, garbanzo beans, hot chili beans, tomatoes, corn, jalapeños and diced green chilies with skillet mixture in slow cooker.
3. Add garlic, chili powder, cumin, parsley, oregano, basil, cilantro, or any seasonings you prefer.
4. Cover and cook on LOW for 6 hours.

Hearty Vegetarian Chili

YIELD 10 bowls I COOK TIME 5 to 6 hours

Ingredients

- 2 T. chili powder
- 1 T. ground cumin
- 1 t. salt
- 2 T. garlic powder
- ¼ c. BBQ sauce
- 1 (8-oz.) can tomato sauce
- 1 (15-oz.) can kidney beans
- 1 (15-oz.) can black beans
- 1 (12-oz.) bag frozen green beans
- 1 (12-oz.) bag frozen corn
- 1 (12-oz.) bag frozen peas
- 1 medium yellow onion, diced
- 1 medium green pepper, chopped
- 1 medium red pepper, chopped
- 1 stalk celery, chopped
- 1 large carrot, chopped
- 1 small zucchini, cubed
- 3 small white potatoes, cubed
- 1 c. water
- 1 large tomato, chunked

Directions

1. Combine all ingredients in slow cooker.
2. Cover and cook on HIGH for 5 to 6 hours, or until vegetables are tender.

Working Mom's BBQ Chili

YIELD 8 bowls **|** **COOK TIME** 8 to 10 hours

Ingredients

½ T. olive oil
1 vidalia onion, chopped
1 ½–2 lb. ground beef
1 large can BBQ grilling beans
1 pack of chili seasoning
Shredded cheese, to garnish
Diced chives, to garnish

Directions

1. In a large skillet, heat olive oil and sauté onion for 1 to 2 minutes.
2. Place beef in skillet with chopped onion and cook until beef is brown.
3. Drain any excess grease.
4. Place beef mixture in slow cooker and mix with remaining ingredients.
5. Cover and cook on LOW for 8 to 10 hours. Top with cheese and chives, if desired.

Say Cheese
Everyone loves classic chili, but presenting it with options can bring a lot to the table. I like to serve this dish alongside macaroni and cheese because the two taste great together. Sometimes I stir the pasta into the soup, while other times I let guests measure their own chili mac and cheese portions.

Chicken and Corn Chili

YIELD 6 bowls **I COOK TIME** 4 to 5 hours

Ingredients

- 1 ½ lb. boneless, skinless chicken breast or ground chicken
- 1 (15-oz.) can black beans, rinsed and drained
- 1 (16-oz.) jar salsa
- 1 t. garlic salt
- 1 t. ground cumin
- 1 t. chili powder
- ¼ t. pepper
- 1 (15 ¼-oz.) can fiesta corn (with red & green peppers)
- Sour cream, to garnish
- Shredded cheddar cheese, to garnish

Directions

1. Place chicken in slow cooker.
2. In a medium bowl, combine drained beans, salsa, garlic salt, ground cumin, chili powder and pepper and place in slow cooker.
3. Cover and cook on LOW for 4 to 5 hours.
4. About 4 hours into cooking, remove chicken and shred with 2 forks. Return chicken to slow cooker and stir.
5. Mix in corn and continue cooking for 30 minutes.
6. Garnish with sour cream and shredded cheddar cheese, if desired.

Add any of your favorite seasonings for more flavor.

Chicken Taco Chili

YIELD 6 to 8 bowls **I COOK TIME** 7 to 7 hours 15 minutes

Ingredients

- 1 medium yellow onion, chopped
- 1 (16-oz.) can black beans
- 1 (16-oz.) can chili-seasoned kidney beans
- 1 (16-oz.) can corn, drained
- 1 (8-oz.) can tomato sauce
- 1 (29-oz.) can diced tomatoes
- 1 (4-oz.) can green chilies
- 1 (1 ¼-oz.) packet taco seasoning
- 2–3 boneless, skinless chicken breasts
- 2 c. shredded Monterey Jack cheese, to garnish
- 1 c. sour cream, to garnish

Directions

1. Combine all ingredients (except garnishes) in slow cooker, adding the chicken last.
2. Cover and cook on LOW for 6 hours 30 minutes.
3. Remove chicken to shred. Add the shredded chicken back into the chili and continue to cook on LOW for 30 to 45 minutes.
4. Serve in bowls topped with cheese, sour cream, tortilla chips or all of the above.

Make your own topper by frying corn tortilla strips.

 # Chickpea Chili

YIELD 8 bowls **I** **COOK TIME** 9 hours 30 minutes

Ingredients

1	c. chickpeas, dried
4	c. water
2	T. coconut oil, divided
1	medium yellow onion, diced
5	garlic cloves, minced
2	T. tomato paste
2	t. ground cumin
1	t. salt
½	t. ground red pepper
½	t. ground cinnamon
¼	t. ground turmeric
1	(24-oz.) container chicken broth
⅔	c. green olives, sliced
½	c. golden raisins
1	(28-oz.) can crushed whole tomatoes
1	large (or 2 lb. frozen) butternut squash, peeled and chopped
1	c. green peas
6	c. cooked couscous, to serve
1	lime, cut into wedges, to garnish
¼	c. chopped cilantro, to garnish

Directions

1. Place chickpeas and water in a saucepan. Bring to a boil, reduce heat and simmer for 1 hour to soften chickpeas. Transfer chickpeas to slow cooker and add just enough water to cover.
2. Heat 1 T. coconut oil over medium. Cook onions until translucent. Add garlic and sauté ingredients for 1 additional minute, stirring constantly.
3. Stir in tomato paste, cumin, salt, red pepper, cinnamon and turmeric. Sauté 30 seconds, stirring constantly.
4. Transfer onion mixture to slow cooker. Combine broth, olives, raisins and tomatoes in a bowl, then pour into slow cooker.
5. Cover and cook on HIGH for 8 hours.
6. Pour remaining coconut oil in skillet and heat over medium-high. Sauté butternut squash and brown for 5 minutes. Transfer squash to slow cooker and stir.
7. Cover and cook on HIGH for 1 hour. Stir in peas and cook for 30 additional minutes on HIGH.
8. If desired, serve over couscous and top with lime and cilantro.

Dad's Famous No-Bean Chili

YIELD 8 to 10 bowls **I** **COOK TIME** 3 to 4 hours

Ingredients

- 3 T. vegetable oil
- 1½ medium onions, chopped
- 1 medium green pepper, chopped
- 1 stalk celery, chopped
- 1 clove garlic, minced
- 1 jalapeño, chopped
- 4 lb. ground beef
  Salt and pepper, to taste
- 8 T. chili powder
- 1 T. ground cumin
- 2 t. garlic salt
- ¼ t. hot sauce
- ½ (12-oz.) bottle beer
- 1¼ c. water
- 1 (14 ½-oz.) can stewed tomatoes
- 1 (8-oz.) can tomato sauce
- 1 (6-oz.) can tomato paste
- 1 (4-oz.) can diced green chilies
- 1 bay leaf

Directions

1. Heat vegetable oil over medium-high and sauté onions, peppers, celery, garlic and jalapeño until vegetables are soft and onions are translucent. Add beef and cook until no longer pink, adding salt and pepper to taste.
2. When finished, spoon away excess oil and transfer beef mixture to slow cooker.
3. In a separate bowl, mix chili powder, cumin, garlic salt, hot sauce, salt, pepper and beer. Let mixture sit before adding to slow cooker.
4. Next, add water, stewed tomatoes, tomato sauce, tomato paste, diced green chilies and bay leaf to slow cooker. Mix well.
5. Cover and cook on LOW for 3 to 4 hours, stirring occasionally. Remove bay leaf before serving.

Soon to be famous among your own family!

 Classic Chili

YIELD 10 bowls **I** **COOK TIME** 5 to 7 hours

Ingredients

- 2 lb. ground turkey or beef
- 2 t. salt
- 1 t. pepper
- 2 (16-oz.) cans kidney beans, drained and rinsed
- 2 (14 ½-oz.) cans diced tomatoes
- 1 (8-oz.) can tomato sauce
- 2 medium yellow onions, chopped
- 1 medium green pepper, chopped
- 2 garlic cloves, minced
- 2 T. chili powder
- 1 t. smoked paprika
- 1 t. ground cumin
  Shredded cheese, to garnish
  Sour cream, to garnish

Directions

1. Heat a large skillet over medium-high. Place ground turkey or beef in the skillet and sprinkle with salt and pepper. Cook until browned.
2. Drain meat on a paper towel, then transfer to slow cooker. Stir in remaining ingredients.
3. Cover and cook on HIGH for 5 hours or LOW for 7 hours.
4. Serve topped with cheese and sour cream, if desired.

 # Pizza Chili

YIELD 6 to 8 bowls **I COOK TIME** 8 hours

Ingredients

1	T. coconut oil
1	lb. ground turkey
1	small white onion, chopped
1	large green pepper, chopped
¼	c. pepperoni, chopped
¼	c. Parmesan cheese, plus more to garnish
1	t. garlic powder
1	T. Italian seasoning
1	t. oregano
1	(15 ½-oz.) can red kidney beans, drained and rinsed
1	(14 ½-oz.) can diced tomatoes, drained
¾	c. water
1	(15-oz.) can tomato sauce
1	T. stevia, to taste
	Chili seasoning, to taste

Directions

1. Heat coconut oil in a large skillet over medium-high. Brown ground turkey with onions and peppers.
2. Add pepperoni during the last 3 to 4 minutes and cook with ground meat.
3. Transfer mixture to slow cooker and stir in Parmesan cheese, garlic powder, Italian seasoning and oregano. Add kidney beans, diced tomatoes, water and tomato sauce. Stir well. Taste, then add sweetener and chili powder, if desired.
4. Cover and cook on LOW for 8 hours.

Even though it's pizza-flavored, this chili is perfect with sour cream.

Pork Chili Verde

YIELD 6 to 8 bowls **I COOK TIME** 6 to 7 hours

Ingredients

- 1 T. olive oil, divided
- 4 boneless pork chops, cut into ½-in. cubes
  Salt and pepper, to taste
- ½ c. chicken broth
- 1 large yellow onion, chopped
- 2 cloves garlic, minced
- 1 T. ground cumin
- 1 T. oregano
- 2 (10-oz.) cans diced tomatoes with green chilies
- 1 (4-oz.) can diced green chilies
- 2 (7-oz.) jars salsa verde
- 1 (14-oz.) can navy beans
  Sour cream, to garnish

Directions

1. Heat oil in a skillet over medium-high. Season pork with salt and pepper, add chops to the skillet and brown both sides. Place browned pork in slow cooker.
2. Heat skillet to medium-high again. Pour in chicken broth and stir to loosen remaining pork in skillet. Add to slow cooker.
3. Add remaining ingredients to slow cooker.
4. Cover and cook on LOW for 6 to 7 hours.
5. Serve topped with sour cream, if desired.

! Playing with Flavors

My family goes crazy for pork in the slow cooker. Not only does pork cook up perfectly, it also absorbs all the additional flavors so well. We love to play with different seasonings and spices to see what kind of great new tastes we can create! You can do the same with this adaptable recipe.

Pumpkin Black Bean Soup

YIELD 10 bowls **I** **COOK TIME** 6 to 7 hours

Ingredients

1	medium yellow onion, chopped
1	medium yellow pepper, chopped
1	medium red pepper, chopped
1	lb. cooked turkey or raw chicken breast, cubed
2	t. garlic powder
1	(30-oz.) can black beans, drained and rinsed
1	(15-oz.) can pure pumpkin
1	lb. pumpkin, peeled and chunked
1	(14 ½-oz.) can diced tomatoes
2	celery stalks, finely chopped
1	T. dried parsley
1	T. chili powder
2	t. ground cumin
1	t. salt
3	c. chicken stock

Directions

1. Place onion and peppers in the bottom of slow cooker. Add chicken or turkey and sprinkle with garlic powder.
2. Add remaining ingredients, pouring chicken stock in last.
3. Cover and cook on LOW for 6 to 7 hours.

Top with sour cream, chives and cheese to make this your new fall favorite!

♨ 🥄 Tomato-Free Chili

YIELD 8 bowls **| COOK TIME** 7 hours

Ingredients

- 3 (15-oz.) cans pinto beans
- 3 (15-oz.) cans great Northern beans
- 2 beef bullion cubes
- 1 c. water
- 1 large green pepper, seeded and diced
- 2 T. chili powder
- 1 large yellow onion, diced
- ½ lb. 85-percent lean ground beef
- ½ lb. ground pork sausage
- 1 T. cornstarch
- ⅓ c. cold water
- 1 t. salt
- Shredded cheese, to garnish

Directions

1. Combine beans, bouillon cubes, water, green pepper and chili powder in slow cooker.
2. Add onion, ground beef and sausage to a large skillet over medium-high heat. Cook just until meat is brown and transfer to a paper towel-lined plate to drain grease. Pour meat mixture into slow cooker.
3. Cover and cook on HIGH for 6 hours. Reduce heat to LOW.
4. Combine cornstarch and cold water and add mixture to slow cooker; add salt.
5. Cover and cook on LOW for 1 hour. Top with shredded cheese, if desired.

❗A New Take

I make a lot of chili in autumn, so I was thrilled to get this recipe from my mother-in-law, Marsha. Making a chili without any tomatoes puts a fresh spin on the classic dish, and it still tastes great. In fact, I think this chili is even better the next day! Just refrigerate and reheat before serving.

Turkey and Sweet Potato Chili

This dish is perfect for a pot luck!

YIELD 6 to 8 bowls **I** **COOK TIME** 8 hours

Ingredients

- 1 medium yellow onion, diced
- 2 garlic cloves, chopped
- 1 (14 ½-oz.) can fire-roasted tomatoes
- 2 large sweet potatoes, peeled and cubed

- 1 (15-oz.) can red beans
- 1 lb. lean ground turkey breast
- 1 bay leaf
- ¾ t. ground cumin
- ⅛ t. salt
- 2 T. chili powder
- 1 ½ c. water

Directions

1. Add all ingredients to slow cooker in the order listed.
2. Cover and cook on LOW for 8 hours.
3. Remove bay leaf and serve.

Turkey and Kale Chili

YIELD 8 to 10 bowls **I** **COOK TIME** 5 to 6 hours

Ingredients

- 1 T. coconut oil
- 1 small yellow onion, chopped
- 2 lb. ground turkey
  Salt and pepper, to taste
- 1 (24-oz.) container chicken broth
- 8 Roma tomatoes, seeded and chopped
- 1 (15-oz.) can dark red kidney beans, drained
- 2 c. kale, chopped
- 1 T. honey
- 2 T. coconut aminos
- 2 T. chili powder
- 2 t. garlic powder
- 1 (6-oz.) can tomato paste
- 1 medium red bell pepper, chopped

Directions

1. Heat coconut oil in a large skillet over medium-high. Add onion and cook for 3 minutes. Next, add turkey and season with salt and pepper. Cook while crumbling with a spatula, until just brown.
2. Transfer turkey mixture to a paper towel-lined plate to absorb grease. Add remaining ingredients to slow cooker. Stir in turkey and onions.
3. Cover and cook on LOW for 5 to 6 hours.

White Chicken Chili

YIELD 7 bowls **I COOK TIME** 8 hours

Ingredients

- 1   T. olive oil
- 3   boneless, skinless chicken breast, cut into ½-in. pieces
- 1   small yellow onion, chopped
- 3   garlic cloves, minced
- 1   (16-oz.) can tomatillo salsa
- 1   (10-oz.) can diced tomatoes with green chilies
- 1   (14 ½-oz.) can chicken broth
- 1   (4-oz.) can diced green chilies
- 1   t. dried oregano
- ½   t. coriander seeds, crushed
- ¼   t. ground cumin
- 2   (15-oz.) cans great northern beans, drained
- 1   T. lime juice
- ½   t. pepper
- ½   c. shredded white cheddar cheese
- 1   T. chopped cilantro

Directions

1. Pour olive oil in a large skillet and heat over medium-high. Add diced chicken and cook for 3 minutes, or until browned.
2. Place chicken in slow cooker with remaining ingredients (except cheese and cilantro).
3. Cover and cook on LOW for 8 hours.
4. Stir in cilantro and serve in bowls topped with white cheddar cheese.

To make this vegetarian, just exclude the chicken.

Mom's Favorite Chili

YIELD 10 bowls **I COOK TIME** 6 to 8 hours

Ingredients

- ½ onion, chopped
- 1 garlic clove, chopped
- 2 lb. ground beef, browned
  Salt and pepper, to taste
- 2–3 T. chili powder
- 1 c. water
- 1 bag pinto beans
- 1 green pepper, diced
- 1 red pepper, diced
- 2 (14.5-oz.) cans diced tomatoes
- 2 (10-oz.) cans Ro*Tel
- 6 oz. tomato sauce

Serve this dish over mashed potatoes for a heartier meal.

Directions

1. Sauté onion and garlic in a skillet over medium-high heat. Add ground beef and season with salt and pepper. Cook until just a bit of pink remains.
2. Meanwhile, mix chili powder with water. Let sit.
3. Transfer meat mixture to a plate lined with a paper towel and drain the fat.
4. Wash and drain beans.
5. Place meat mixture in slow cooker. Pour beans over meat mixture and top with water/ chili powder mixture. Put remaining ingredients in the slow cooker and mix well. Make sure beans are covered with liquid. Cover and cook on LOW for 6 to 8 hours.

Southwestern Turkey Chili

YIELD 4 to 6 bowls **I** **COOK TIME** 6 hours

Ingredients

- 2 lb. ground turkey, lean
- 1 vidalia onion, chopped
- 1 t. minced garlic
- 1 red pepper, chopped
- 1 ½ c. corn, frozen
- 4 (14-oz.) cans diced tomatoes
- 1 T. smooth peanut butter
- 1–2 (15-oz.) cans kidney beans, rinsed and drained
- 1 packet chili seasoning mix
  Salt and pepper, to taste
  Shredded cheese, to garnish

Directions

1. Brown turkey, onion and garlic in a skillet over medium-high heat just until pink coloring is gone.
2. Drain fat by spooning meat mixture onto a plate covered with paper towels and place a paper towel on top to soak up any grease.
3. Place drained meat mixture into slow cooker. Add in remaining ingredients and stir well. Cover and cook on LOW for 6 hours. Serve topped with shredded cheese, if desired.

Make It Your Own

One of the things I like best about chili is how customizable it can be. I make this particular chili with ground turkey, but you can make it with any meat you like! Chili traditionalists can use beef, but you can also substitute the turkey for ground chicken. Whatever you choose, you won't be disappointed!

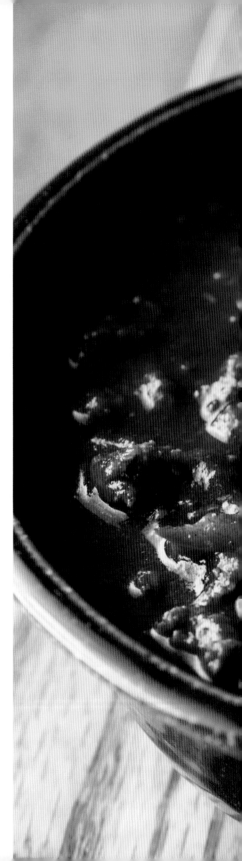

 # Pumpkin Chicken Chili

YIELD 6 bowls **I** **COOK TIME** 6 to 8 hours or 4 to 5 hours

Ingredients

- 1 (14-oz.) can tomatoes, diced
- 2 c. chicken broth
- 1 (14-oz.) can pumpkin puree
- 1 large onion, diced
- 5 garlic cloves, minced
- 1 T. chili powder
- 1 t. ground cumin
- 1 t. coriander
- 1 t. kosher salt
- ¼ t. pepper
- 1–2 chipotle peppers in adobo sauce, seeds removed, minced (optional)
- 1 ½ lb. chicken breasts or cutlets, skin and visible fat removed
- 1 (28-oz.) can chickpeas, rinsed and drained
- 1 c. corn kernels, if frozen, thawed
- 1 red bell pepper, diced
- 1 green bell pepper, diced
- 2 T. fresh cilantro, chopped
  Sour cream, shredded cheddar, guacamole/avocado, green onions and/or tortilla chips, for serving

Directions

1. Add tomatoes, chicken broth and pumpkin to slow cooker.
2. Whisk pumpkin mixture until well combined. Add onion, garlic, chili powder, cumin, coriander, salt, pepper and chipotles and stir.
3. Add chicken, chickpeas, corn, red bell pepper and green bell pepper. Cover and cook for 6 to 8 hours on LOW or for 4 to 5 hours on HIGH.
4. When ready to serve, remove chicken and chop into bite-size pieces or shred with two forks.
5. Add chicken back to pot. Stir in cilantro and serve topped with sour cream, shredded cheddar, green onions, guacamole and/ or tortilla chips, if desired.

Chili Colorado

YIELD 12 bowls **I COOK TIME** 6 to 8 hours

Ingredients

- 9 dried red chilies
- 3 c. water
- 5 lb. beef chuck roast
- ½ c. all-purpose flour
- 1 T. kosher salt
- 1 T. pepper
- 3 T. olive oil
- 1 large yellow onion, chopped
- 2 t. minced garlic
- 2 c. beef broth or water
- 2 t. cumin
- ½ t. cayenne pepper
  White rice, to serve

Directions

1. Bring chilies and water to boil in a medium pan.
2. Remove from heat and let steep for 30 minutes. Strain cooking liquid to reserve. Transfer chilies and some liquid into a blender and puree.
3. Strain sauce through a fine mesh strainer; set aside. Trim fat from chuck roast, and cut into 2-in. chunks.
4. Combine flour, salt and pepper in a bowl. Coat beef chunks in the seasoned flour and set aside.
5. Place olive oil in a large skillet over medium heat and sauté garlic and onion for 4 to 5 minutes until tender and translucent.
6. Place beef chunks in skillet and cook to evenly brown.
7. Transfer beef to slow cooker and add remaining seasons
8. Increase heat to medium-high and deglaze skillet by pouring in beef broth. Scrape up brown bits, transfer liquid to slow cooker.
9. Add pureed sauce, cover and cook on LOW for 6 to 8 hours. Serve over white rice.

Chili Con Carne

YIELD 20 bowls **I** **COOK TIME** 4 to 5 hours or 8 to 10 hours

This recipe can be halved easily to serve a smaller crowd.

Ingredients

- 1 lb. dried red kidney beans
- 4 lb. ground beef
- 2 c. onion, chopped
- 2 garlic cloves
- 5 T. chili powder
- 3 beef bouillon cubes, crushed
- 2 t. smoked paprika
- 1 t. oregano
- 1 t. ground cumin
- ½ t. cayenne pepper
- 4 (14.5-oz.) cans beef stock
- 1 (56-oz.) can crushed tomatoes
- 1 (6-oz.) can tomato paste
- 1 medium red bell pepper
- ½ c. chopped celery

Directions

1. Soak red kidney beans overnight, rinse and clean.
2. Brown ground beef with salt and pepper in skillet and discard fat.
3. Place a liner in slow cooker. Combine all ingredients in the liner, stirring well. Cover and cook on LOW for 8 to 10 hours or HIGH for 4 to 5 hours.

Famous Cincinnati Chili

YIELD 6 bowls **I COOK TIME** 6 hours

Ingredients

1 ½ lb. lean ground beef
2 medium onions, chopped
6 garlic cloves, minced
½ c. chopped celery
2 T. chili powder
1 T. paprika
1 ½ t. dried basil
1 ½ t. dried oregano
1 t. dried thyme
1 t. ground cinnamon
½ t. cayenne pepper
½ t. ground cumin
½ t. crushed red pepper flakes
¼ t. ground allspice
½ t. salt
½ t. pepper
1 (29-oz.) can tomatoes, diced
1 (8-oz.) can tomato sauce
½ c. water
1 lb. spaghetti (optional)
1 (15-oz.) can red kidney beans (optional)

Directions

1. In a large skillet, brown ground beef, onions and garlic, drain off all excess fat.
2. Transfer all ingredients into the slow cooker and stir well.
3. Cover and cook on LOW for 6 hours.
4. Switch slow cooker to WARM setting and cook spaghetti according to package directions. .

Top with a splash of hot sauce for an extra kick!

Fire-Roasted Black Bean Chili

YIELD 6 bowls **I** **COOK TIME** 6 hours

Ingredients

- 1   T. oil
- 1   medium white onion, chopped
- 3   garlic cloves, minced
- 3   celery stalks, chopped
- 1   lb. ground beef
    Salt and pepper, to taste
- 1   medium green or red pepper, seeded and chopped
- 1   (14.5-oz.) can black beans
- 1   (28-oz.) can fire roasted crushed tomatoes
- 1   (14.5-oz.) can fire roasted diced tomatoes with green chilies
- 2   t. cumin
- 3   T. chili powder
- ½   t. oregano
- 1   c. beef broth or water
    Sour cream, shredded cheese, diced onions (optional, for garnish)

Directions

1. Place oil in skillet and heat over medium.
2. Sauté onions, garlic and celery until onions are translucent.
3. Add ground beef, salt and pepper and cook until just a bit of pink color remains.
4. Drain beef/onion mixture on a paper towel lined plate to absorb grease.
5. Transfer mixture to slow cooker. Add remaining ingredients and stir.
6. Cover and cook on LOW for 5 hours. Taste and adjust seasonings, then cook for 1 additional hour on LOW.
7. Serve with toppings such as diced onions, shredded cheese or sour cream.

Serve with a side of tortilla chips for a winning combination!

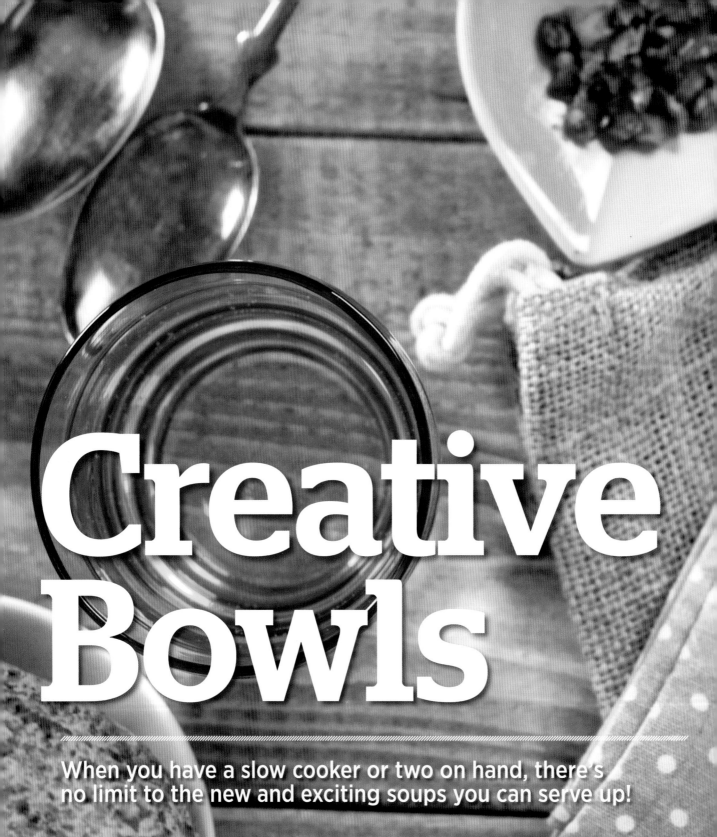

Creative Bowls

When you have a slow cooker or two on hand, there's no limit to the new and exciting soups you can serve up!

Bacon and broccoli are a match made in heaven!

15-Bean Sausage Soup

YIELD 8 to 10 bowls **I COOK TIME** 5 to 7 hours

Creative Bowls

Ingredients

- 1 (16-oz.) pkg. dried 15-bean soup mix
- 1 lb. ground or sliced Italian sausage
- 1 medium yellow onion, chopped
- 1 (28-oz.) container chicken broth
- 2 bay leaves
- ½ t. Italian seasoning
- 1 small bunch kale, torn into bite-sized pieces
- 3 carrots, peeled and chopped
- 3 cloves garlic, minced
- 1 (15-oz.) can stewed tomatoes

Directions

1. Sort, rinse and soak beans overnight, or for about 8 hours.
2. Brown ground sausage and onion in a skillet over medium-high heat. Drain fat and transfer mixture to slow cooker. Stir in all remaining ingredients (except tomatoes).
3. Cover and cook on HIGH for 2 hours. Turn slow cooker to LOW and cook for 3 to 5 hours, or until beans are tender. About 1 hour before finished cooking, add stewed tomatoes.
4. Remove bay leaves and serve.

Healthier Options

You can always make this soup a little bit healthier to satisfy different diets by substituting a couple ingredients. Instead of using Italian sausage, you can make this soup taste just as great with ground turkey. The chicken broth can also be swapped out for vegetable broth.

 # Albondigas Soup

YIELD 8 bowls **I COOK TIME** 8 hours

Ingredients

- 3 large carrots, peeled and sliced
- 3 stalks celery, thinly sliced
- 24 meatballs, uncooked
- ½ t. chopped mint
- 1 t. salt
- ½ t. pepper
- 1 t. minced garlic
- 1 (14 ½-oz.) can diced tomatoes
- ¼ c. marinara sauce
- 4 c. chicken broth
- 1 ½ c. white rice, cooked

Directions

1. Place carrots and celery in slow cooker. Add meatballs, mint, salt, pepper and garlic. Stir in tomatoes, marinara sauce and chicken broth.
2. Cover and cook on LOW for 8 hours.
3. Stir in cooked rice and serve in individual bowls.

Either homemade or frozen meatballs will work.

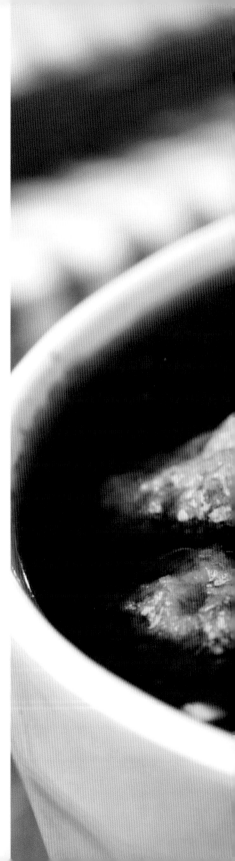

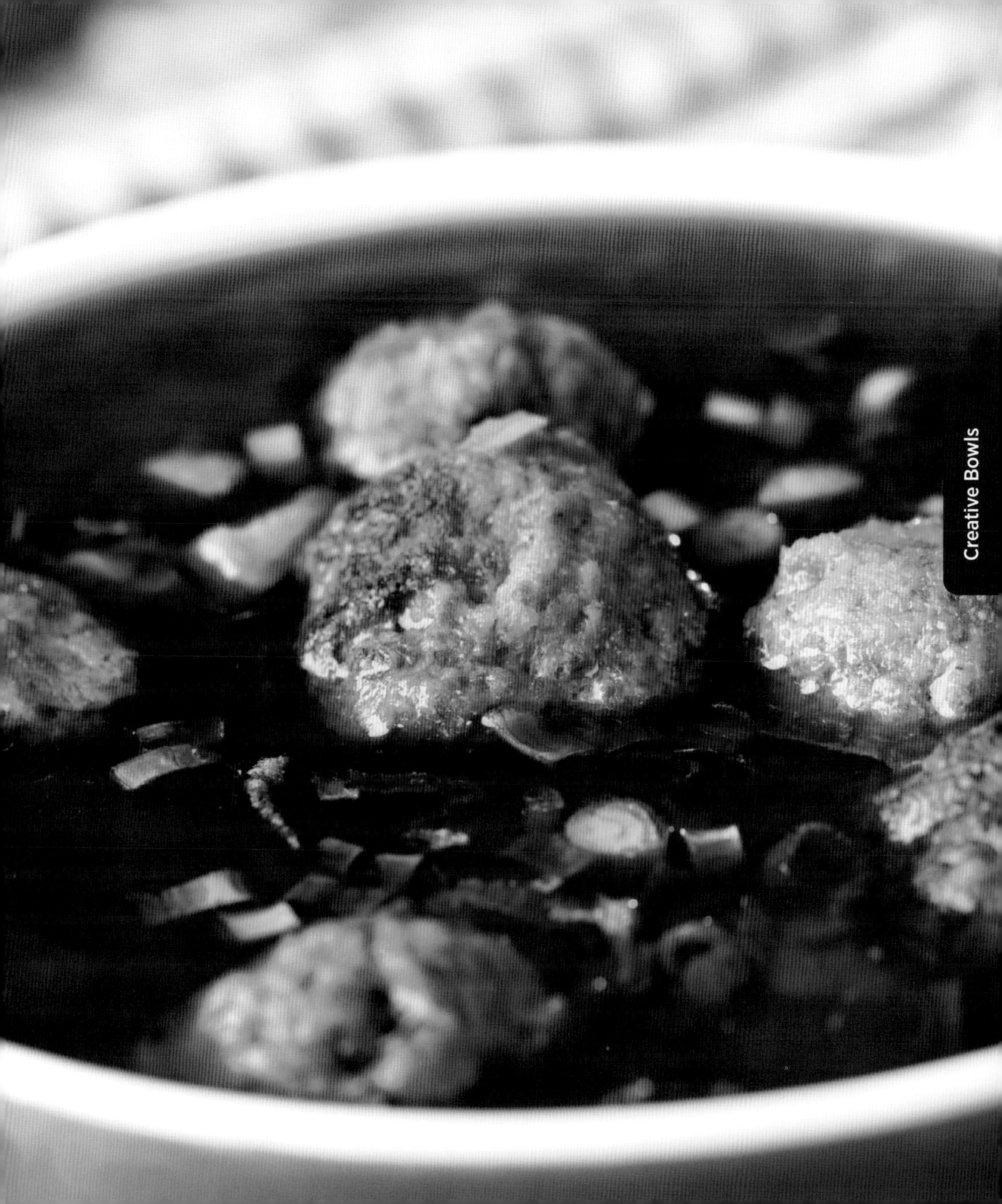

 # Brown Jug Soup

YIELD 10 to 12 bowls **I COOK TIME** 10 to 12 hours

Ingredients

ROUX

3	T. unsalted butter
3	T. flour
¼	t. poultry seasoning
¼	t. sage
¼	t. salt
1	dash pepper
½	c. chicken broth
½	c. water

SOUP

1	(32-oz.) container chicken broth
1	c. water
4	stalks celery, chopped
2	medium yellow onions, diced
4	medium potatoes, peeled and diced
8	large carrots, peeled and julienned
1	(10-oz.) pkg. frozen whole kernel corn
½	lb. Velveeta cheese, cubed

Directions

ROUX

1. Melt butter in a saucepan over medium heat. Stir in flour and cook until it begins to turn a golden brown. Sprinkle in poultry seasoning, sage, salt and pepper. Stir in chicken broth and water. Cook until thickened, about 5 minutes, stirring frequently.

SOUP

1. Add roux, chicken broth, water, celery, onions, potatoes, carrots and corn to slow cooker. Stir to combine.
2. Cover and cook on LOW for 10 to 12 hours, or until the vegetables are tender.
3. Stir in cheese and serve soup when melted.

Cheddar Bratwurst Soup

YIELD 6 to 8 bowls **I COOK TIME** 4 hours 15 minutes to 6 hours 15 minutes

Ingredients

- 1   T. olive oil
- 1   small yellow onion, chopped
- 2   cloves garlic, minced
- 6   medium red potatoes, cubed
- 2   large carrots, peeled and chopped
- 1   green onion, sliced
- 1   T. unsalted butter
- 4   bratwursts, uncooked, sliced
- ½   t. salt
- ¼   t. pepper
- ½   t. dry ground mustard
- 1 ½ c. shredded cheddar cheese
- 4   c. chicken stock
- 1   (12-oz.) bottle ale beer
- ¼   c. water
- 2   T. cornstarch
- 1   c. half-and-half

Directions

1. Heat olive oil in a skillet over medium. Add yellow onion and garlic. Cook until onions are brown and tender.
2. Place potatoes, carrots and green onions in slow cooker. Top with skillet mixture.
3. Add butter and brats to the heated skillet and brown over medium heat. Drain grease and add brats to slow cooker. Add salt, pepper, mustard and cheese. Top with chicken stock and beer.
4. Cover and cook on HIGH for 4 hours or on LOW for 6 hours.
5. Combine water with cornstarch and stir mixture into the soup, along with the half-and-half.
6. Cover and cook on HIGH for 15 minutes.

Dumpling Soup

YIELD 5 bowls | **COOK TIME** 4 hours 30 minutes to 6 hours 30 minutes

Serving vegetarians? Just skip the steak!

Ingredients

- 1 lb. round steak, cut into 1-in. cubes
- ½ (2-oz.) packet French onion soup mix
- 3 c. hot water
- 2 large carrots, peeled and shredded
- 1 stalk celery, chopped
- 1 medium tomato, diced
- 1 c. spinach
- 1 c. biscuit mix
- 1 T. dried Italian seasoning
- 6 T. milk

Directions

1. Place steak in slow cooker and sprinkle with dry onion soup mix. Add water, carrots, celery, tomato and spinach.
2. Cover and cook on LOW for 4 to 6 hours, or until steak cubes are tender.
3. Turn slow cooker to HIGH.
4. In a separate bowl, combine biscuit mix and Italian seasoning. Stir in milk with fork until mixture is moistened. Drop mixture into slow cooker by the teaspoonful.
5. Cover and cook on HIGH for 30 minutes.

Egg Drop Soup

YIELD 8 bowls **I** **COOK TIME** 4 hours 45 minutes to 6 hours 45 minutes

Ingredients

- 3 boneless, skinless chicken thighs
- 8 c. chicken broth
- ½ t. minced ginger
- 1 garlic clove, minced
- 1 (4-oz.) package mushrooms, diced
- 3 green onions, sliced
- 2 T. tamari or coconut aminos
- 3 T. rice vinegar
  Salt and pepper, to taste
- 3 eggs plus 1 egg yolk

Directions

1. Place chicken, chicken broth, ginger, garlic and mushrooms in slow cooker.
2. Cover and cook on HIGH for 4 hours or on LOW for 6 hours.
3. Remove chicken and shred. Set aside. Stir in green onions, tamari, rice vinegar, salt and pepper.
4. Cover and cook on LOW for 30 minutes.
5. Whisk eggs in a small bowl, then slowly pour into slow cooker. Do not stir.
6. Cover and cook on LOW for 15 minutes.
7. Serve soup in individual bowls over shredded chicken.

Serve with a side of rice for a complete meal.

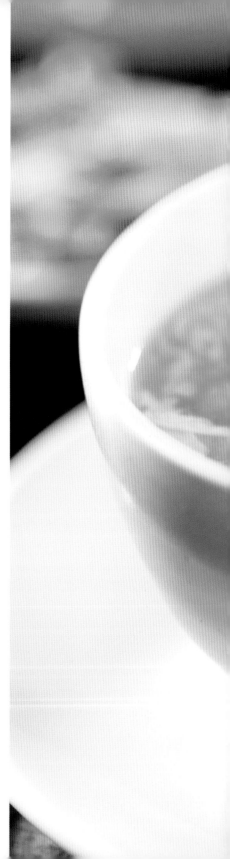

Enchilada Soup

YIELD 6 bowls **I** **COOK TIME** 8 hours

Ingredients

- 1 lb. ground beef, browned and drained
- 1 medium yellow onion, sliced
- 1 (15-oz.) can pinto beans with liquid
- 1 (15-oz.) can whole kernel corn
- 1 (15-oz.) can stewed Mexican style tomatoes
- 2 (8-oz.) cans enchilada sauce
- 1 (8-oz.) package Mexican style shredded cheese
- 1 small bag tortilla chips

Directions

1. Place all ingredients (except the cheese and chips) in slow cooker.
2. Cover and cook on LOW for 8 hours.
3. Serve in individual bowls topped with cheese and chips.

Add Avocado

My favorite way to top off this enchilada soup is with a nice slice of avocado. Many Mexican dishes are garnished with this delicious and healthy fruit, and I find that it adds a nice creaminess to the soup. Plus, avocados always make a great garnish thanks to their bright green color!

 # Hamburger Lentil Soup

YIELD 6 bowls **I COOK TIME** 8 hours

Ingredients

½ lb. ground beef
1 c. dried lentils
1 (28-oz.) can diced tomatoes
1 (15-oz.) can kidney beans
3 stalks celery, sliced
3 large carrots, peeled and sliced
1 small yellow onion, diced
1 t. minced garlic
1 (24-oz.) container beef broth
1 t. dried basil
1 t. dried oregano
½ t. dried thyme
2 bay leaves

Directions

1. Brown ground beef in a large skillet. Drain fat.
2. Combine all ingredients in slow cooker.
3. Cook on LOW for 8 hours.
4. Serve immediately or, for best flavor, refrigerate soup overnight. Add 1 c. beef broth and reheat to serve.

Extra veggies lying around? Add them in! Corn, other beans and green beans make great additions to this versatile dish!

Kansas City Steak Soup

YIELD 6 to 8 bowls **I** **COOK TIME** 9 hours 15 minutes

Ingredients

- 1 (32-oz.) container beef broth
- 1 large yellow onion, chopped
- 3 stalks celery, chopped
- 6 medium tomatoes, chopped
- 2 medium potatoes, peeled and cubed
- 2 carrots, peeled and sliced
- ½ t. pepper
- 1 t. salt
- 1 (10-oz.) package frozen mixed vegetables
- 1 lb. round steak, browned and cubed
- ½ c. butter
- ½ c. flour

Directions

1. Add all ingredients (except the butter and flour) to slow cooker.
2. Cover and cook on LOW for 9 hours. Turn slow cooker to HIGH.
3. While soup is cooking, melt butter in a saucepan over medium heat. Stir in flour and cook for about 5 minutes, until golden brown in color. Add the mixture to slow cooker and stir well to combine.
4. Cover and cook on HIGH for 15 minutes.

Serve this soup over some fresh-from-the-oven biscuits for a heartier (and delicious!) meal.

≋ ✐ Hot and Sour Soup

YIELD 10 bowls **I** **COOK TIME** 6 hours 30 minutes

Ingredients

- 1 c. shiitake mushrooms
- 1 (14-oz.) can bamboo shoots, sliced
- 2 carrots, julienned
- 2 green onions, sliced
- 1 (32-oz.) container vegetable broth
- ¼ c. rice vinegar
- ¼ c. soy sauce or coconut aminos
- 2 T. minced fresh ginger
- 1 T. minced garlic
- 1 T. hot sweet chili sauce
- Salt and white pepper, to taste
- ¼ c. cold water
- 3 T. cornstarch
- 1 c. firm tofu, cubed
- 1 pkg. French fried onions, to garnish

Directions

1. Place all ingredients except tofu, water, cornstarch and French fried onions in slow cooker.
2. Cover and cook on LOW for 6 hours.
3. In a small bowl, combine cornstarch and water to dissolve. Add to slow cooker.
4. Stir tofu into soup.
5. Cover and cook for 30 additional minutes on LOW.
6. Serve in individual bowls topped with French fried onions.

 # Pasta e Fagioli

YIELD 13 bowls **I** **COOK TIME** 5 hours 30 minutes to 8 hours 30 minutes

Ingredients

- 2 lb. 90-percent lean ground beef
- 1 medium yellow onion, chopped
- 3 large carrots, peeled and chopped
- 4 stalks celery, chopped
- 2 (28-oz.) cans diced tomatoes
- 1 (16-oz.) bag red kidney beans, rinsed and drained
- 1 (16-oz.) can white kidney beans, rinsed and drained
- 2 (14 ½-oz.) containers beef stock
- 3 t. oregano
- 2 t. pepper
- 5 t. parsley
- 1 t. Tabasco sauce
- 1 (24-oz.) jar marinara sauce
- 1 (8-oz.) package pasta

Directions

1. Brown beef in a skillet. Drain fat from beef and add to slow cooker with everything except pasta.
2. Cover and cook on LOW for 7 to 8 hours or HIGH for 5 to 6 hours.
3. Add pasta of your choice and cook for 30 additional minutes.

Use a cheese-filled pasta to make this a meal.

Creative Bowls

Peanut Butter Pumpkin Soup

YIELD 4 to 6 bowls **I COOK TIME** 2 hours 15 minutes to 3 hours 30 minutes

Ingredients

- ¼ c. diced onion
- 2 c. pumpkin puree
- 1 t. paprika
- 2 T. butter
- 2 c. chicken broth
- ⅛ c. creamy peanut butter
- ¼ c. half-and-half
- Sour cream, to garnish
- Salt and pepper, to taste

Directions

1. Place onions, pumpkin puree, paprika, butter and chicken broth in slow cooker.
2. Cover and cook on LOW for 2 to 3 hours, or until soup is smooth.
3. After 3 hours, heat peanut butter and half-and-half in a saucepan. Whisk until smooth then stir into slow cooker.
4. Cook another 15 to 30 minutes and serve hot with a dollop of sour cream on top. Season to taste with salt and pepper.

Love savory and sweet flavors? This is the soup for you!

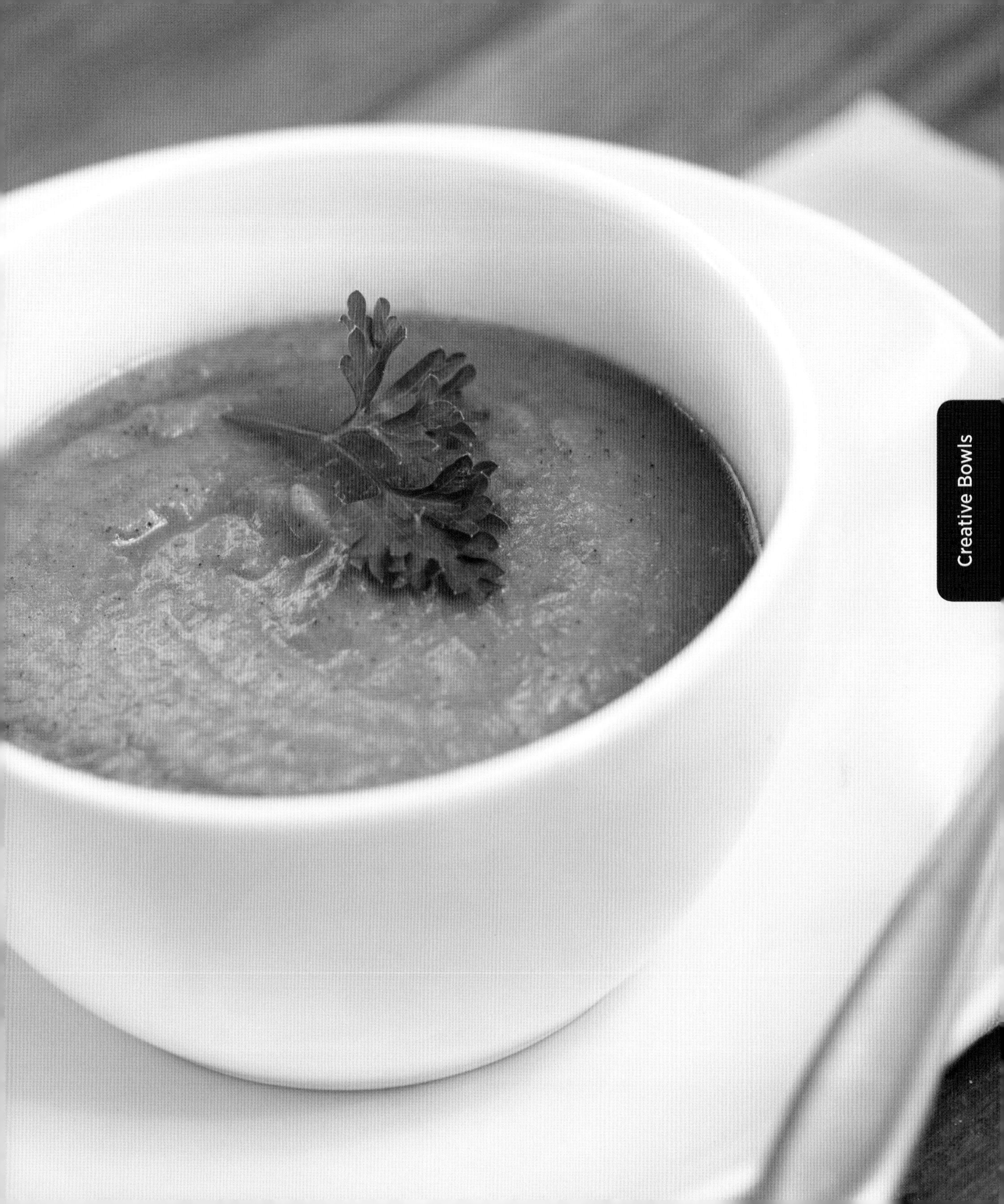

♨ 🥄 Zuppa Toscana

YIELD 4 to 6 bowls **I COOK TIME** 3 to 4 hours

Ingredients

- 1   lb. sausage
- 1   (16-oz.) container chicken broth
- 4   c. water
- 2   garlic cloves, minced
- 2   large russet baking potatoes, halved and cut into ¼-in. slices
- 1   large yellow onion, chopped
- 2   c. kale or Swiss chard, chopped
- 1   c. heavy whipping cream

Directions

1. Brown sausage in a skillet over medium-high heat. Transfer sausage to slow cooker with broth, water, garlic, potatoes and onions.
2. Cover and cook on HIGH for 3 to 4 hours, or until potatoes are cooked and soft. If desired, mash potatoes.
3. Turn off the slow cooker, add kale and cover for 5 minutes. Stir in whipping cream and serve.

✎ Best Breadsticks

🥄 This Italian soup tastes just like one you'd get at a fancy restaurant, so I like to serve it with a worthy side: garlic breadsticks! Whether you choose to make homemade breadsticks or buy pre-made, the topping is key. Mix 2 T. butter with ½ t. garlic and brush on the bread before serving. Yum!

Leftover Turkey Noodle Soup

YIELD 4 to 6 bowls **I** **COOK TIME** 4 hours 30 minutes to 5 hours

Ingredients

- 2 c. cooked turkey, cut into bite-sized chunks
- 1 small onion, chopped
- 1 carrot, chopped
- 2 celery stalks, chopped
- 4 c. water
- 4 c. turkey broth
- 1 t. seasoned salt
- 1 t. salt
- ¼ t. pepper
- 1 bay leaf
- 6 oz. noodles of your choice

Directions

1. Place all ingredients except noodles in slow cooker. Cover and cook on LOW for 4 hours.
2. Remove bay leaf and add noodles. Cover and cook for another hour on LOW or 30 minutes on HIGH until noodles are soft.

15-Bean Corned Beef Stew

YIELD 12 bowls **|** **COOK TIME** 8 hours

Ingredients

- 1   (20-oz.) pkg. 15-bean soup
- 3   lb. corned beef
- 1   onion, chopped
     Salt and pepper, to taste
- 3   garlic cloves, whole
- 1   can of dark beer

Directions

1. Rinse and sort beans. Place beans in slow cooker and cover with 3 c. of water. Cover and cook on LOW for 7 hours.
2. Meanwhile, prepare corned beef.
3. Place corned beef in a separate slow cooker. Top beef with chopped onion, salt, pepper and whole garlic cloves.
4. Pour beer over top. Cover and cook on LOW for 6 hours.
5. When beef is finished, remove from slow cooker and shred. Reserve the liquid.
6. Place shredded corned beef in the slow cooker containing the beans; stir.
7. Pour reserved liquid from corned beef slow cooker over top beans and beef. Stir to combine well. Cover and cook on LOW for 1 hour.
8. Serve hot with cornbread or side of your choice.

Serve this soup to celebrate St. Patrick's Day!

Smashed Potato Soup

YIELD 8 bowls **I** **COOK TIME** 6 hours 30 minutes to 8 hours 30 minutes

Ingredients

- 3 lb. Klondike potatoes, cubed
- 1 yellow onion, diced
- 2 green chilies, peeled, deseeded and chopped
- 1 t. minced garlic
  Salt and pepper, to taste
- 1 (32-oz.) container chicken broth
- ½ c. sour cream
- 12 oz. sharp cheddar cheese, shredded, plus more for garnish
- 4 oz. frozen broccoli
- 12 pieces cooked bacon, crumbled
- 4 green onions, sliced

Directions

1. Place diced potatoes, yellow onion, chilies, garlic, salt, pepper and chicken broth in slow cooker.
2. Cover and cook on LOW for 6 to 8 hours.
3. Carefully use a hand blender and slightly whip soup to break up potatoes into smaller pieces.
4. Add sour cream, cheese and broccoli.
5. Cover and cook for an additional 30 minutes on LOW. Top with bacon, green onions and cheese when serving.

Add either fresh or frozen corn to give this soup even more color and flavor.

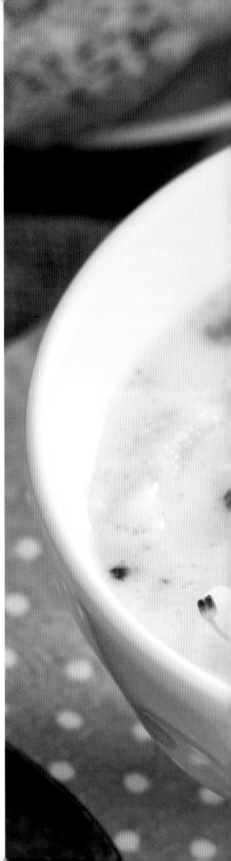

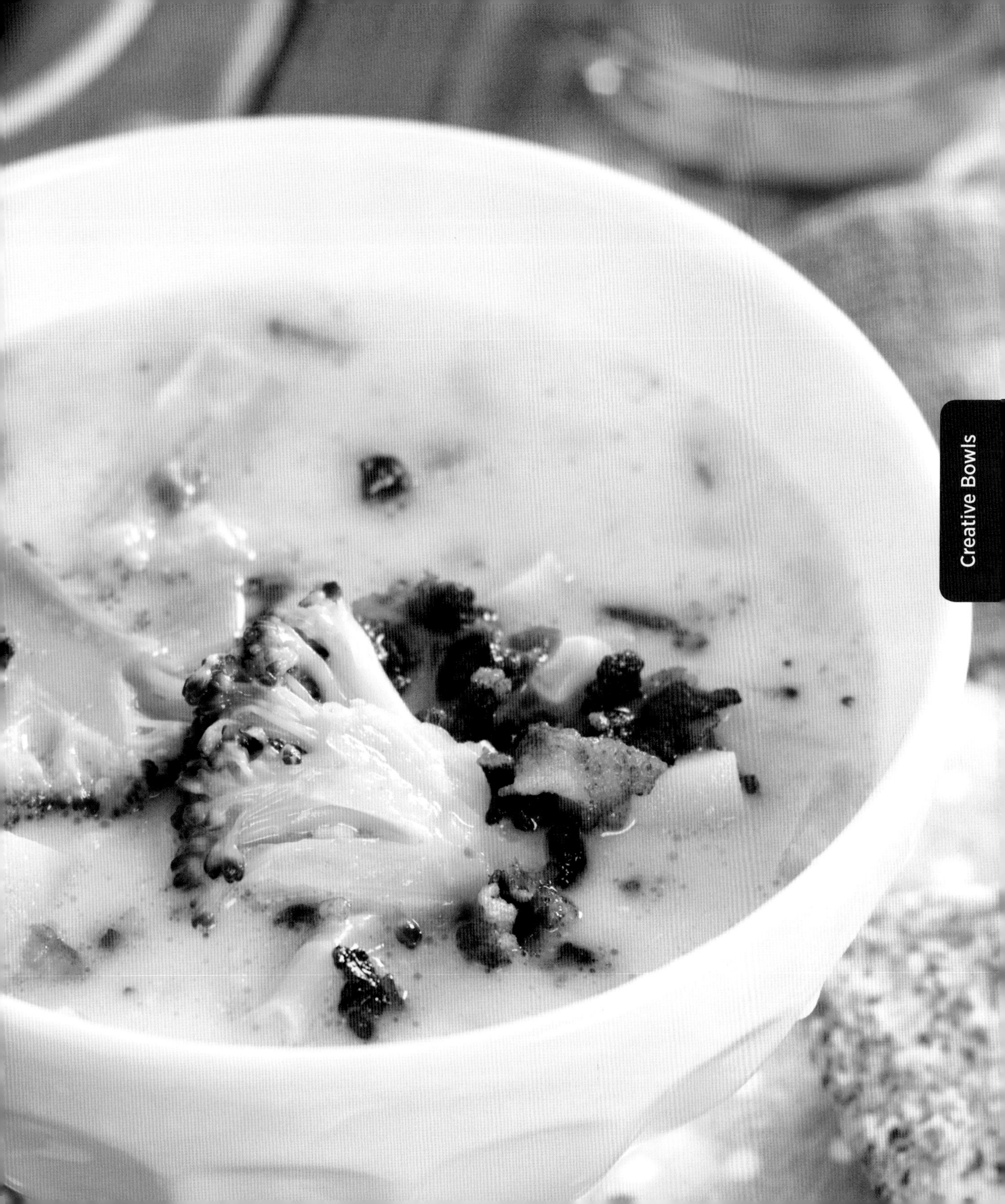

 # Savory Turkey and Dumpling Soup

YIELD 4 to 6 bowls **I COOK TIME** 4 hours 30 minutes to 7 hours

Ingredients

- 2–3 c. cooked turkey, roughly chopped
- 1 (14.5-oz.) can petite tomatoes, diced
- ½ c. diced onion
- ½ c. diced carrots
- 2 celery ribs, sliced
  Salt, to taste
- 1 T. poultry herb blend
- 1 (12-oz.) can condensed cream of chicken soup
- 2–2 ½ c. chicken broth
- 1 (8-oz.) can crescent roll dough or biscuit dough

Directions

1. Add turkey and vegetables to slow cooker. Season with salt and herb blend. Cover all with condensed soup and broth. Cover and cook on LOW 4 to 6 hours.
2. Meanwhile, form raw dough into small balls and add to top of soup mixture after 4–6 hour mark.
3. Cover and cook on HIGH another 30 to 60 minutes, or until dough has started to cook.

A great use of all that leftover turkey you happen to have on hand!

 # Lasagna Soup

YIELD 8 bowls **I** **COOK TIME** 6 to 7 hours

Ingredients

- 1 lb. bulk Italian sausage, cooked and drained
- 1–2 large onions, diced
- 5 garlic cloves, minced
- 1 T. dried oregano
- 1 T. dried basil
- ¼ t. red pepper flakes
- 1 (6-oz.) can tomato paste
- 1 (28-oz.) can fire-roasted tomatoes
- 2 bay leaves
- 6 c. chicken broth
  Salt and pepper, to taste
- 10 oz. lasagna noodles, broken into pieces
  Ricotta and mozzarella cheeses, for topping

Directions

1. Combine all ingredients except lasagna noodles and cheeses in slow cooker.
2. Cover and cook on LOW for 6 to 7 hours.
3. During the last 30 minutes, add uncooked pasta.
4. Top with cheese and serve.

If desired, broil in oven-safe bowl for 3 to 5 minutes to brown cheese.

 # Taco Soup

YIELD 8 bowls **I COOK TIME** 8 hours

Ingredients

- 1 lb. ground beef
- 1 onion, chopped
- 1 (1 ¼-oz.) pkg. taco seasoning mix
- 1 (1-oz.) pkg. ranch seasoning mix
- ¼ c. water
- 1 (15-oz.) can kidney beans, with liquid
- 1 (15-oz.) can corn whole kernel, with liquid
- 1 (8-oz.) can tomato sauce
- 2 c. water
- 1 (28-oz.) can diced tomatoes
- 1 (4-oz.) can green chili peppers, diced
  Hot sauce, to taste

Directions

1. Brown ground meat with onion, taco seasoning, ranch seasoning and water over medium heat. Drain and set aside.
2. Transfer ground meat mixture from the skillet along with the kidney beans, corn, tomato sauce, hot sauce, diced tomatoes and green chili peppers to slow cooker.
3. Stir to blend. Cover and cook on LOW for 8 hours.

Bean Soup with Leftover Ham Bone

YIELD 9 to 10 bowls **I** **COOK TIME** 8 hours

Ingredients

- 1 (20-oz.) pkg. 15-bean soup
- 1 ham bone
- 1 onion, sliced
- 1 carrot, peeled and chopped
- 1 celery stalk, chopped
- 6 c. chicken broth
- 2 bay leaves
- 2 garlic cloves, minced
- 2 T. honey
  Salt and pepper, to taste

Directions

1. Drain canned beans and place in slow cooker. Add remaining ingredients and stir. Cover and cook on LOW for 8 hours.
2. Remove ham bone and pull meat off the bone. Remove bay leaves.
3. Add ham back to soup and stir.

 # Day After Turkey Soup

YIELD 8 to 10 bowls **I COOK TIME** 7 hours

Ingredients

Turkey carcass, skin and meat removed

1 onion, quartered or chopped

2–3 carrots, peeled, halved or chopped

3 celery stalks, chopped

2–3 rosemary sprigs

Small handful black peppercorns

2 bay leaves

2 qt. chicken broth

Salt, to taste

3 c. leftover turkey meat

2 c. pasta or rice

Top with leftover stuffing to make this a day-after dish to delight.

Directions

1. Place turkey carcass in slow cooker. Arrange onion quarters, carrot, celery, rosemary bundle, black peppercorns and bay leaves in slow cooker. Cover with chicken broth.

2. Cover and cook on HIGH for 4 hours. Next, strain broth into colander, with bowl underneath to capture broth. Set veggies aside. Rinse slow cooker.

3. Pour broth back into slow cooker; add chopped carrots, chopped celery, chopped onion, salt and turkey meat.

4. Cover and slow cook on LOW for 3 hours more.

5. Thirty minutes before serving, remove carcass and then add pasta or rice.

Steak Diane Mushroom Stew

YIELD 6 bowls **I COOK TIME** 4 to 5 hours to 8 to 10 hours

Ingredients

- 2 medium onions, cut in wedges
- 2 garlic cloves, minced
- 3 c. sliced fresh button mushrooms
- 1 ½ lb. beef round steak, boneless, trimmed and cut in 1-in. cubes
- 1 (14.1-oz.) can organic cream of mushroom soup, condensed
- ¼ c. tomato paste
- 2 t. Worcestershire sauce
- 1 t. dry mustard
- ½ t. cracked black pepper
- 2 green onions, sliced
- 3 c. noodles, hot cooked

Directions

1. Place onions topped with garlic and mushrooms in slow cooker. Transfer steak to top of onions and mushrooms.
2. In a separate bowl, combine remaining ingredients except noodles and stir well.
3. Pour over steak in slow cooker. Cover and cook on LOW for 8 to 10 hours, or on HIGH for 4 to 5 hours.
4. Prepare noodles before serving, according to directions on package.

You can also add any of your favorite steak sauces to this dish before serving.

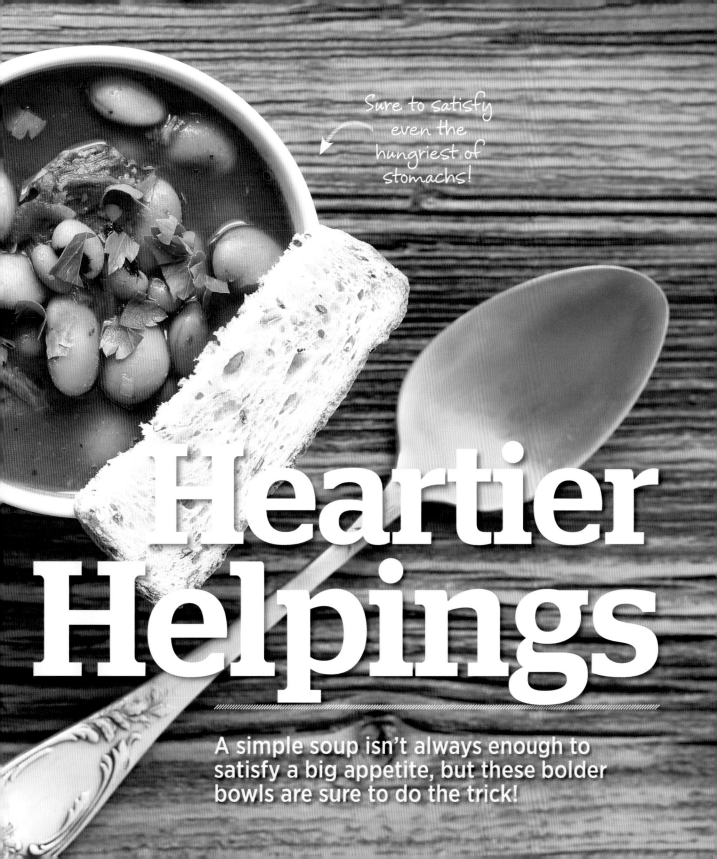

Sure to satisfy even the hungriest of stomachs!

Heartier Helpings

A simple soup isn't always enough to satisfy a big appetite, but these bolder bowls are sure to do the trick!

# Chicken Gumbo

YIELD 6 to 8 bowls | **COOK TIME** 6 hours

Ingredients

4	T. butter
2	T. all-purpose flour
1	medium yellow onion, chopped
2	cloves garlic, minced
1	medium green pepper, seeded and chopped
2	ribs celery, chopped
1	c. chopped okra
2	lbs. chicken breast
½	t. garlic powder
1	t. dried thyme
1	t. dried basil
1	bay leaf
½	t. cayenne pepper
¼	t. sea salt
¼	t. black pepper
32	oz. chicken stock
1	T. cornstarch plus ¼ c. water
8	c. cooked rice

Directions

1. Make a roux with the butter and flour in a skillet over medium heat. Stir constantly until thickened and dark brown (do not burn!).
2. Add onions and garlic to skillet and cook just until onion starts to turn translucent.
3. Place vegetables in slow cooker.
4. Top with chicken breast, seasonings, the roux and chicken stock.
5. Combine cornstarch and water in a small bowl until dissolved. Pour into slow cooker.
6. Cover and cook on LOW for 6 hours.
7. Carefully remove chicken breast and chop into bite-sized pieces. Return to slow cooker and stir.
8. Remove bay leaf.
9. Serve gumbo over hot white rice. Sprinkle with additional salt and pepper, if desired.

Buffalo Chicken 15 Bean Soup

YIELD 10 bowls **I** **COOK TIME** 5 to 6 hours

Ingredients

- 1 (20-oz.) pkg. 15-bean soup
- 1 c. diced carrot
- 1 c. diced onion
- 1 c. diced celery
- 2 lb. boneless, skinless chicken breasts (raw)
- 8 c. chicken stock
- 1 c. Buffalo sauce
  Blue cheese crumbles, to garnish

Directions

1. Rinse and sort beans. Check for unwanted debris and discard.
2. In slow cooker, add rinsed beans, carrot, onion, celery, chicken breast, bean flavor packet and chicken stock.
3. Cover and cook on HIGH for 5 to 6 hours.
4. Remove and shred chicken, then add back to slow cooker.
5. Pour in buffalo sauce and stir to combine.
6. Keep warm until ready to serve. Top with blue cheese crumbles, if desired.

Heartier Helpings

Great for Games

When my husband settles in for game day, he loves to snack on anything involving buffalo chicken. So, instead of making the standard buffalo chicken dip every time, I like to mix it up by making this soup sometimes. The best part about it? You can still use it to dip tortilla chips in!

 # Chicken and Wild Rice Soup

YIELD 10 bowls **I COOK TIME** 7 to 8 hours

Ingredients

1	c. wild rice
3	boneless, skinless chicken breasts
2	stalks celery, chopped
1	medium yellow onion, chopped
2	large carrots, julienned
1	(4-oz.) pkg. mushrooms, sliced
1	(48-oz.) container chicken stock
1	t. thyme
1	t. sage
½	c. unsalted butter
¾	c. flour
2	c. milk
3	T. white wine

Directions

1. Rinse and drain uncooked wild rice, then transfer to slow cooker. Add chicken, celery, onion, carrots, mushrooms, chicken stock and seasonings.
2. Cover and cook on LOW for 7 to 8 hours.
3. When cooking is nearly finished, melt butter in a saucepan over medium heat. Add flour and let the mixture bubble for 1 minute. Slowly whisk in milk to form a thick, creamy mixture. Stir in wine.
4. Remove chicken and shred or chunk. Add meat back into slow cooker with the skillet mixture, stir and serve.

If desired, stir in rice vinegar instead of wine.

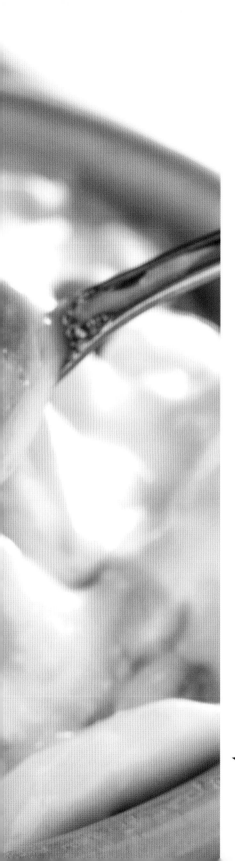

Chicken Corn Chowder

YIELD 8 bowls I **COOK TIME** 5 to 6 hours

Ingredients

- 2   T. butter
- 4   boneless, skinless chicken breasts, cut into ½-in. pieces
- 1   small yellow onion, chopped
- 2   stalks celery, sliced
- 2   small carrots, sliced
- 1   c. frozen corn
- 1   c. frozen peas
- 2   small potatoes, cubed
- 1   c. frozen green beans
- 2   (10 ¾-oz.) cans cream of potato soup
- 1 ½   c. chicken broth
- 1   t. dried dill weed
- ½   c. half-and-half or evaporated milk

Directions

1. Melt butter in a large skillet over medium heat. Add chicken and cook until charred. Transfer chicken to slow cooker, then add onion and celery to the skillet. Sauté for 3 to 4 minutes, or until tender.
2. Add onions and celery to slow cooker, along with carrots, corn, peas, potatoes, green beans, soup, chicken broth and dill.
3. Cover and cook on LOW for 5 to 6 hours, or until vegetables are tender.
4. During the last 10 minutes, stir in half-and-half or evaporated milk.

You can replace butter with coconut oil for a healthier alternative.

Heartier Helpings

Chicken Gnocchi Soup

YIELD 4 to 6 bowls **I** **COOK TIME** 5 hours 20 minutes

Ingredients

- 4 T. unsalted butter
- 2 T. olive oil
- 1 medium yellow onion, diced
- 3 stalks celery, sliced
- 2 garlic cloves, minced
- ¼ c. flour
- 1 (14-oz.) container chicken broth
- ½ t. dried thyme
- 1 t. salt
- ½ t. pepper
- 2 large carrots, shredded
- 4 boneless, skinless chicken breasts, cut into ½-in. pieces
- 1 c. chopped spinach
- 4 c. half-and-half
- 1 (16-oz.) pkg. gnocchi, cooked

Directions

1. Heat butter and oil in a large skillet over medium-high. Add onion, celery and garlic and cook until onion is translucent. Sprinkle in flour and whisk. Cook 1 minute, stirring occasionally. Stir in chicken broth and seasonings.
2. Transfer skillet mixture to slow cooker, then add carrots and chicken.
3. Cover and cook on LOW for 5 hours.
4. Stir in the spinach and half-and-half. Cover and cook on LOW for another 20 minutes while you prepare gnocchi according to package directions.
5. Stir the gnocchi into soup and serve in individual bowls.

This soup also tastes great with tortellini pasta. Just swap in for the gnocchi and follow the same directions.

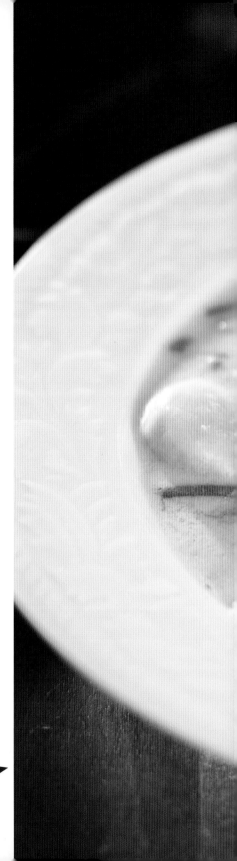

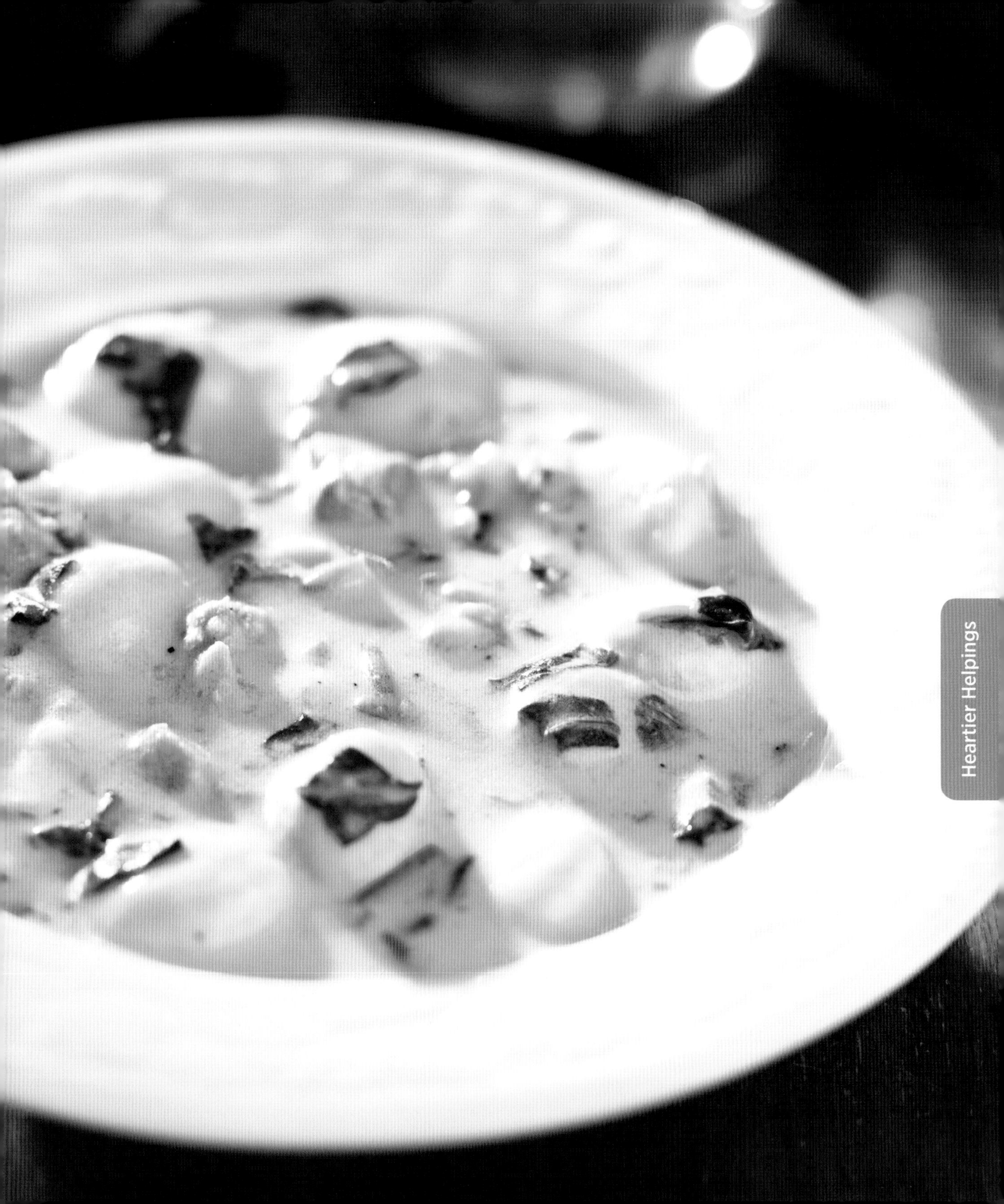

Chicken Tortilla Soup

YIELD 8 bowls **|** **COOK TIME** 3 to 4 hours or 6 to 8 hours

Ingredients

3	boneless, skinless chicken breasts
1	(15-oz.) can crushed tomatoes
1	(10-oz.) can enchilada sauce
1	medium yellow onion, chopped
1	(4-oz.) can diced green chilies
2	garlic cloves, minced
2	c. water
1	(14 ½-oz.) can chicken broth
1	t. ground cumin
1	t. chili powder
1	t. salt
¼	t. pepper
1	bay leaf
1	(10-oz.) bag frozen corn
1	T. chopped cilantro
½	lime, juiced
1	small bag tortilla chips

Directions

1. Add chicken, tomatoes, enchilada sauce, onion, green chilies and garlic to slow cooker. Add water, chicken broth, cumin, chili powder, salt, pepper and bay leaf. Stir in corn and cilantro.
2. Cover and cook on LOW for 6 to 8 hours or on HIGH for 3 to 4 hours.
3. Remove chicken and shred, then return to slow cooker. Add lime juice and stir.
4. Serve in bowls and top with crushed tortilla chips.

Round out this dish with a dollop of sour cream.

Easy
Mexican Chicken Soup

YIELD 4 to 5 bowls | **COOK TIME** 3 to 4 hours or 5 to 6 hours

Ingredients

- 1 medium yellow onion, diced
- 1 red bell pepper, seeded and sliced
- 3 boneless, skinless chicken breasts
- 1 T. chili powder
- 2 t. ground cumin
- 1 t. oregano
- 1 t. salt
- 1 c. tomatillo sauce or salsa verde
- 2 garlic cloves, minced
- 2 c. chicken broth

Directions

1. Layer onion and bell pepper in the bottom of slow cooker. Add chicken breast, chili powder, ground cumin, oregano and salt.

2. Add tomatillo sauce or salsa verde, garlic and chicken broth.

3. Cover and cook on LOW for 5 to 6 hours or on HIGH for 3 to 4 hours.

Harvest Chicken Soup

YIELD 6 to 8 bowls **I** **COOK TIME** 4 to 6 hours

Ingredients

- 1   bay leaf
- 1   sprig fresh thyme
- 3-4 peppercorns
- 1   cheesecloth
- 4   c. chicken stock
- 1   rotisserie chicken breast, shredded
- 2   T. butter
- 2   large carrots, peeled and chopped
- 2   medium potatoes, chopped
- 3   celery stalks, chopped
- 1   t. minced garlic
- ⅛   t. minced ginger
- 1   medium yellow onion, chopped
- 1   medium zucchini, chopped
- 2   yellow squash, chopped
- 3   mushrooms, sliced
    Salt, to taste

Directions

1. Tie bay leaf, thyme and peppercorns together in a bundle with a piece of cheesecloth.
2. Place remaining ingredients in slow cooker. Add the cheesecloth bouquet.
3. Cover and cook on LOW for 6 hours or on HIGH for 4 hours
4. Remove bouquet and serve.

For firmer mushrooms, add in the last hour of cooking.

Healthier Chicken Soup

YIELD 8 bowls **I** **COOK TIME** 6 to 7 hours

Ingredients

4	bone-in, skinless chicken breasts
4	c. water
4	c. low-sodium chicken broth
1	t. sea salt
¼	t. pepper
1	small yellow onion, finely diced
2	medium carrots, peeled and chopped
2	stalks celery, chopped
1	bay leaf
1	(6-oz.) pkg. pasta of your choice
1	bundle fresh herbs, such as rosemary and thyme

Directions

1. Place all ingredients (except noodles and fresh herbs) in slow cooker.
2. Cover and cook on LOW for 5 to 6 hours.
3. Discard bay leaf. Remove and shred or chunk chicken, then return to slow cooker.
4. Add noodles and bundled fresh herbs and cook on LOW for 1 hour, or until noodles are done to your liking.

Great for Guests

Finding the perfect dish to serve a group of guests can be difficult because everyone has different dietary needs and preferences. That's why I always recommend this soup! Not only is it a healthy option, it can also satisfy those who follow a paleo diet who you may be serving!

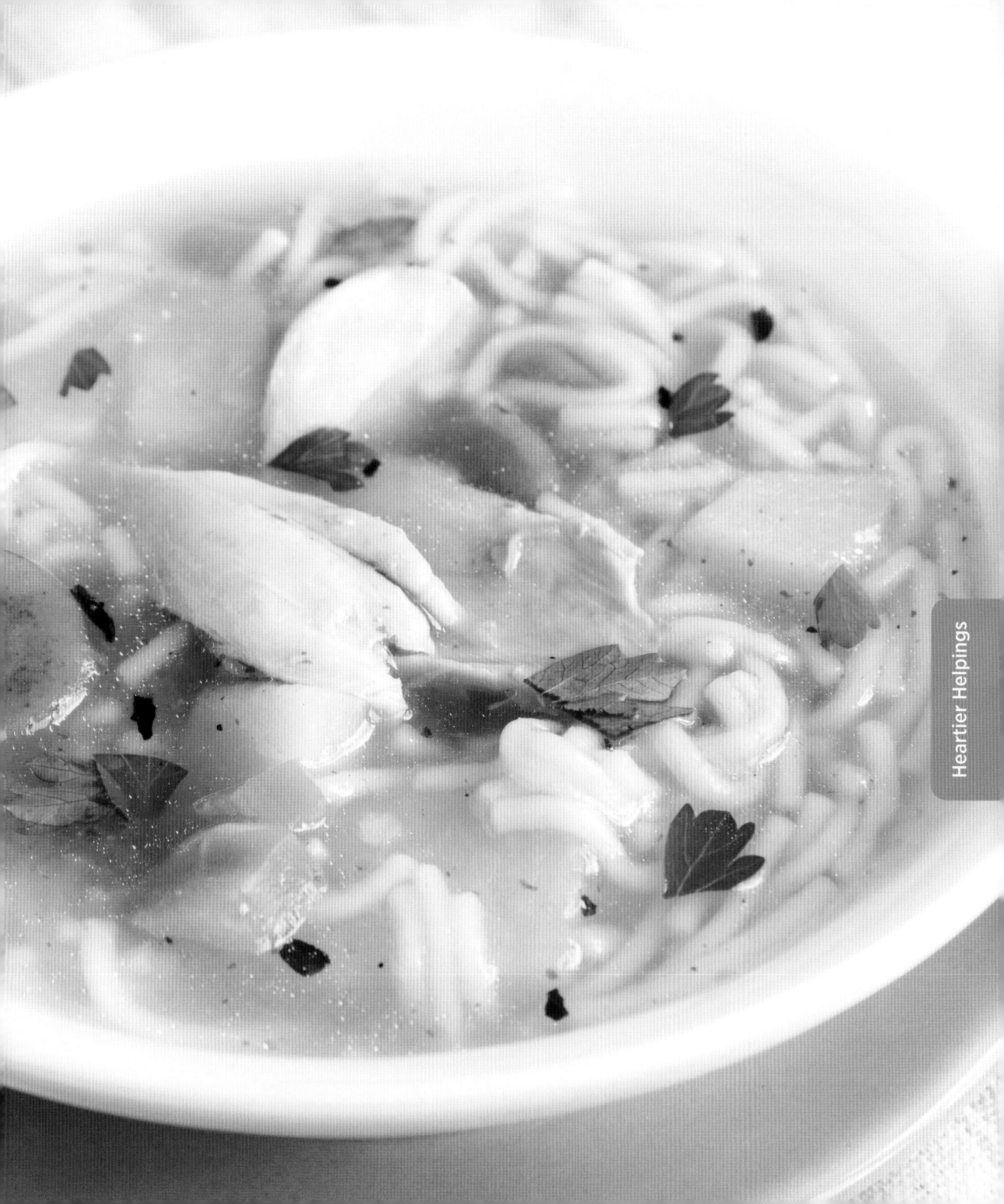

 # Pork Posole

YIELD 8 to 10 bowls **|** **COOK TIME** 5 to 6 hours

Ingredients

SLOW COOKER 1

2	lb. pork shoulder, cut into 1 ½-in. pieces
1 ⅔	c. chopped onion
1 ½	t. ground cumin
1 ½	t. salt
5	c. water
2	cubes chicken bouillon
4–6	thai red chili peppers, whole
14	oz. red sauce, frozen

SLOW COOKER 2

1 ½	lb. dry Northern beans, rinsed and washed
2	lb. fresh nixtamal corn, rinsed and well drained
1 ½	t. salt
6	c. water

Sometimes, it takes two slow cookers to make one great dish.

Directions

1. Soak beans overnight or for several hours for slow cooker 2.
2. Combine pork, onion, cumin, salt, water, chicken bouillon, red chili peppers and red sauce in slow cooker 1.
3. Cover slow cooker 1 and cook on LOW for 5 to 6 hours.
4. Combine Northern beans, nixtamal corn, salt and water in slow cooker 2.
5. Cover slow cooker 2 and cook on LOW for 5 to 6 hours.
6. When both cookers are ready, stir pork and red chili peppers ONLY from slow cooker 1. Remove and discard chili peppers (set aside about 4 c. of red chili sauce/broth from slow cooker). Once chili peppers are removed and sauce is set aside, combine pork mixture from slow cooker 1 with corn and beans in juice in slow cooker 2.
7. Add about 2–3 c. red sauce/broth until desired flavor is reached.
8. Keep in slow cooker on warm until ready to serve.
9. Garnish with fresh cut cilantro, lemon or lime wedges, green onion and/or avocado (cubed).

Paleo
Lamb Stew

YIELD 6 bowls **|** **COOK TIME** 7 to 8 hours

Ingredients

- 1 large yellow onion, sliced
- 2 lb. lamb shoulder meat, cut in 1-in. cubes
- 1 (14-oz.) can diced green chilies
- 1 (14 ½-oz.) can diced tomatoes
- 1 T. minced garlic
- 2 t. oregano
- 1 t. pepper
- 1 t. sea salt
- 1 t. dried thyme
- ½ t. cardamon
- 1 t. ground cumin
- 1 T. chili powder
- 3 c. free-range chicken stock
- 2 T. red wine vinegar
- 8 oz. mushrooms, quartered
- ½ c. chopped cilantro, to garnish

Directions

1. Place sliced onions in bottom of slow cooker.
2. Top onions with cubed lamb.
3. In a medium bowl, combine chilies, diced tomatoes, garlic and seasonings. Pour over lamb in slow cooker.
4. Add chicken stock and vinegar.
5. Top with mushrooms.
6. Cover and cook on LOW for 7 to 8 hours.
7. Serve in bowls and garnish with freshly chopped cilantro, if desired.

If you don't love lamb, try this with grass-fed beef.

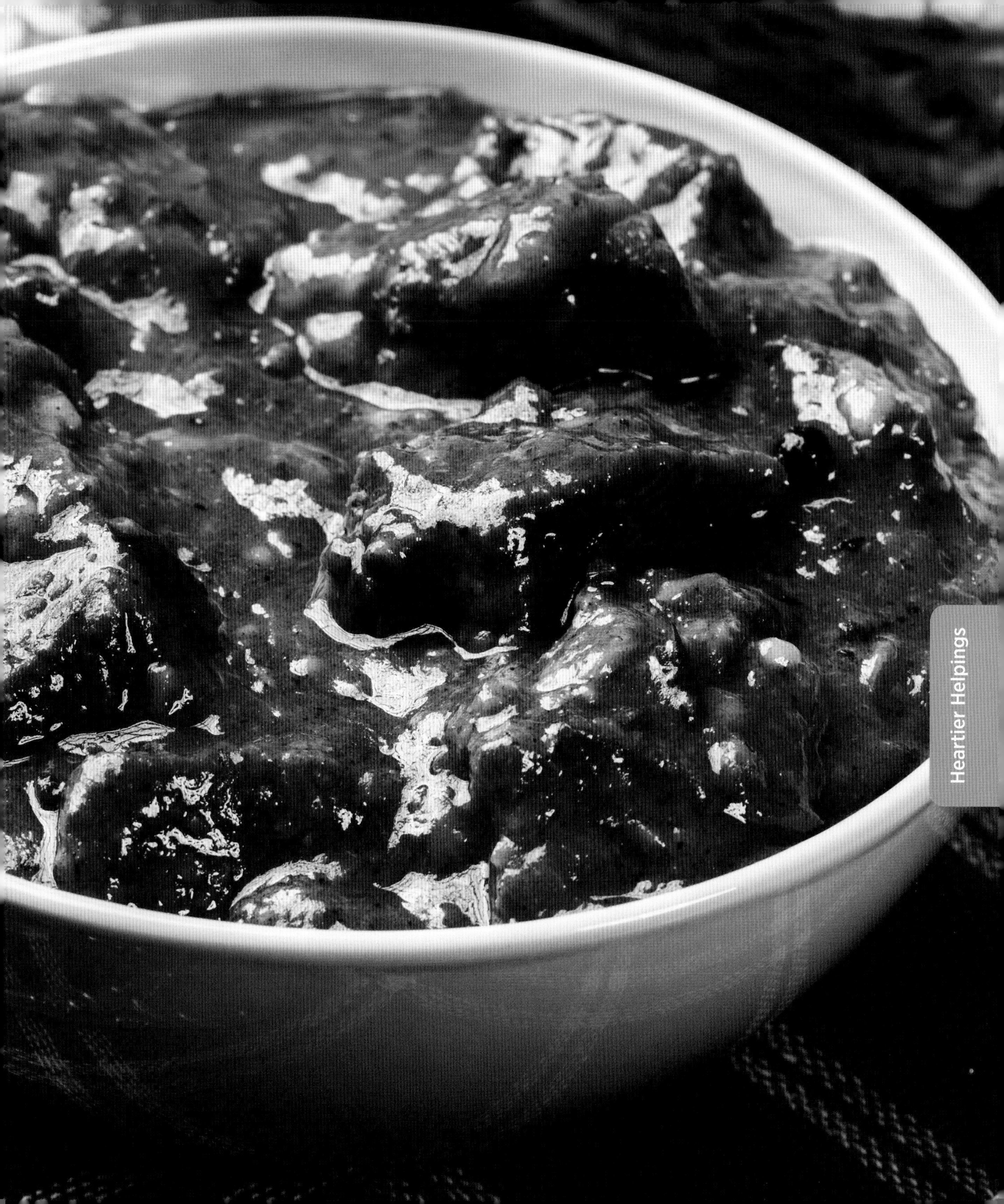

 Veal Stew

YIELD 4 bowls **| COOK TIME** 7 to 8 hours

Serve over noodles, rice or with risotto.

Ingredients

- 2   T. coconut oil
- 2   T. all-purpose flour
- ½   t. salt
- ¼   t. pepper
- 1   lb. veal shoulder, roast, cubed
- 4   carrots, peeled and chopped
- ½   c. beef broth
- 1   large onion, finely chopped
- 1   small red pepper, cut in strips
- 2   medium garlic cloves, minced
- 1   (14 ½-oz.) can diced tomatoes
- ⅛   t. ground sage
- ¼   t. dried oregano, crushed
-     Mushrooms (optional)
-     Rosemary, to garnish

Directions

1. Heat coconut oil in a large skillet over medium-high heat.
2. Mix flour, salt and pepper in a shallow dish.
3. Dredge the veal through the flour mixture and sear on both sides in skillet or just until there is a nice brown finish.
4. Place carrots in slow cooker and top with veal.
5. Carefully pour ¼ c. beef broth into hot skillet, scraping up any browned bits. Pour into cooker along with remaining beef broth.
6. Add onions, red pepper, garlic and diced tomatoes to slow cooker.
7. Add sage and oregano. If desired, add mushrooms.
8. Cover and cook on LOW for 7 to 8 hours.
9. Serve topped with rosemary, if desired.

Cajun
15-Bean Soup

YIELD 10 bowls **|** **COOK TIME** 5 hours

Ingredients

- 1 pkg. Cajun 15-bean aoup, seasoning packet set aside
- 1 yellow onion, diced
- 1 green bell pepper, diced
- 1 c. diced celery
- 2 cloves chopped garlic
- 4 c. chicken stock
- 4 c. water
- 1 lb. Andouille smoked sausage, sliced into ¼-in. rounds
- 1 can stewed or diced tomatoes

Directions

1. Rinse and sort beans, discard any unwanted debris.
2. Add rinsed beans, onion, pepper, celery, garlic, chicken stock, water and seasoning packet into slow cooker.
3. Stir to combine everything.
4. Cover and cook on HIGH for 5 hours.
5. After 5 hours, check beans for doneness. If tender, add sausage and tomatoes.
6. Cook for at least an additional 30 to 45 minutes, keep warm until ready to serve.
7. Serve with long grain rice or fresh cornbread.

 # Paleo
Beef Shank Soup

YIELD 6 bowls **I** **COOK TIME** 2 to 4 hours

Ingredients

- 1 lb. beef shank on bone
  Sea salt and pepper, to taste
- 4 c. beef stock
- 4 c. water
- 2 sweet potatoes, quartered
- 2 carrots, peeled
- 2–4 celery stalks, thickly sliced
- 4 garlic cloves, chopped
- 1 onion, quartered
- 1 large parsnip

Directions

1. Season beef with sea salt and pepper. If desired, lightly sear beef in a skillet for a few minutes on each side.
2. Place beef shank, broth, water, sweet potatoes, carrots, celery, garlic and onion into slow cooker.
3. Place parsnips on top of liquid.
4. Cover and cook on LOW for 4 hours or on HIGH for 2 hours.

Veggie Variety

When you're making a hearty soup such as this one, you can never have too many veggies. I like to toss in just about any additional veggies I have on hand when I make this soup, such as tomatoes and green and red bell peppers. But make sure they're organic to keep it paleo!

Heartier Helpings

Fall Harvest Chowder

YIELD 8 to 10 bowls **I** **COOK TIME** 7 to 8 hours

Ingredients

- 1 lb. ground turkey, browned and drained
- ½ c. onion, chopped
- 4 c. water
- 3 carrots, peeled and chopped
- 3 ribs celery, chopped
- 2 medium potatoes, peeled and cubed
- 2 (14-oz.) cans tomatoes, diced
- 1 t. salt
- ¼ t. pepper
- 1 T. Italian seasoning
- 1 (32-oz.) container chicken broth
- 1 bay leaf
- Parsley, to garnish

Directions

1. Place onion, carrots, celery and potatoes in slow cooker, then top with remaining ingredients.
2. Cover and cook LOW for 7 to 8 hours.
3. For thicker chowder, combine 1 T. corn starch and ¼ c. water then stir into slow cooker. Cook an additional 30 minutes with lid off.
4. Serve in a bread bowl, garnished with fresh grated Parmesan cheese and fresh grated parsley.

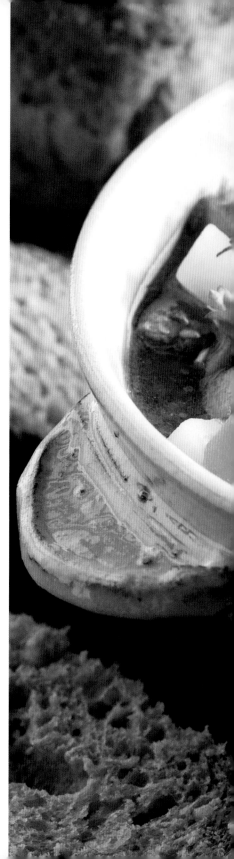

Edible Bowls

When the weather starts to get increasingly cooler, I tend to like my soups and chowders accompanied by plenty of bread. So, when I make this delicious autumn dish, I don't serve it with a side of bread, I serve it right in a bread bowl! Trust me, your guests will certainly support this decision!

Easy, Loaded
Bratwurst Stew

YIELD 4 bowls **|** **COOK TIME** 6 to 7 hours

Ingredients

- 1 lb. bratwurst, cooked and cut into bite-sized pieces
- 4 c. cabbage, sliced
- 5 small red potatoes, chopped (do not peel)
- 1 large red pepper, diced
- 1 medium white onion, diced
- 1 T. Dijon mustard
- 1 T. cider vinegar
- ¼ t. salt
- ¼ t. pepper
- 3 ½ c. chicken broth
- ½ c. beer
- ½ c. provolone or Swiss cheese

Directions

1. Combine all ingredients except cheese in slow cooker.
2. Cover and cook on LOW for 6 to 7 hours.
3. If desired, serve in bowls with provolone or Swiss cheese on top of stew.

Garnish with parsley instead of cheese, if you prefer.

Pot Roast Slow Cooker Stew

YIELD 6 bowls | **COOK TIME** 8 hours 15 minutes

Ingredients

- 2 ½ lb. boneless beef chuck shoulder
- 2 c. onion, chopped
- 1 (14 ½-oz.) can tomatoes with green peppers and onions, diced, undrained
- 1 c. frozen hash brown potatoes, cubed
- 1 c. carrots, diced
- 1 c. beef broth
- 1 T. garlic, minced
- 4 oz. mushrooms
- 1 t. thyme leaves, dried
- ½ t. salt
- ¼ t. pepper
- ½ c. frozen peas

Directions

1. Cut beef shoulder into 2-inch cubes. Place in slow cooker.
2. Add onions, tomatoes, potatoes, carrots, broth, garlic, mushrooms, thyme, salt and pepper. Stir in with beef.
3. Cover and cook on LOW for 8 hours.
4. Stir in frozen peas; cover and cook on LOW for 15 additional minutes.

Add more broth to make this dish a little more soupy.

 ## Cajun
15-Bean Stew

Let guests add their favorite hot sauce.

YIELD 8 to 10 bowls **|** **COOK TIME** 8 hours

Ingredients

- 1 (20-oz.) pkg. Cajun 15-bean soup
- 2 carrots, peeled and sliced
- ½ large white onion, sliced
- 3 pieces of bacon, cooked and crumbled
- 2 celery stalks, chopped
- 3 cloves garlic, minced
- 1 (14-oz.) can diced tomatoes
- 3 c. beef broth
  Hot sauce, to taste
  Salt and pepper, to taste
- 1 pkg. smoked sausage, sliced
  Rice (optional)

Directions

1. Rinse beans and place in slow cooker. Add enough water to cover beans by about 5–6 inches. Soak overnight.
2. Drain beans and return to slow cooker.
3. Add remaining ingredients to slow cooker except sausage and rice. Stir well to combine.
4. Cover and cook on LOW for 8 hours.
5. With about 1 hour of cook time remaining, slice sausage and brown in a skillet over medium-high heat. Transfer to slow cooker.
6. Continue cooking until beans have cooked for 8 hours and are nice and soft.
7. Remove about 1 c. beans and transfer to a food processor or blender. Pulse to puree and return to slow cooker.
8. Stir all ingredients to combine. Taste, add a bit of hot sauce if needed.
9. Serve as a stew or over rice.

New Year's Day Soup

YIELD 8 bowls **I** **COOK TIME** 3 to 4 hours or 6 to 8 hours

Ingredients

- 1 ½   lb. ground sausage
- 1   large onion, chopped
- 2   minced garlic cloves
- 3   (15 ½-oz.) cans black eyed peas, rinsed and drained
- 2 ½   c. chopped cabbage
- 1   c. chopped carrots
- 2   c. water
- 2   (14 ½-oz.) cans stewed tomatoes
- 1   (10-oz.) can Ro*Tel tomatoes
- 1   T. beef bouillon, granules
- 1   T. molasses or honey
- 1   t. Worcestershire sauce
- ½   t. salt
- ¼   t. pepper
- ¼   t. ground cumin

Directions

1. Brown sausage along with onion and garlic in skillet.
2. Transfer to slow cooker, and add all remaining ingredients and mix well.
3. Cover and cook on LOW for 6 to 8 hours or on HIGH for 3 to 4 hours.

Barbecue
Beef Stew

YIELD 4 to 6 bowls **I COOK TIME** 9 hours

Ingredients

5	new potatoes, chopped
3	carrots, chopped
2	lb. stewing beef, cut into chunks
1	medium onion, chopped
1	small green pepper, chopped
1	T. minced garlic
2	T. olive oil
¼	c. red wine
1	t. coarse salt
½	t. pepper
16	oz. beef broth
1	(14 ½-oz.) can stewed tomatoes
6	oz. white mushrooms, washed and quartered
⅓	c. barbecue sauce
¼	c. water
3	T. cornstarch
1	(14.5-oz) can green beans

Directions

1. Add potatoes and carrots to bottom of slow cooker.
2. Brown meat in a skillet over medium-high heat and set on top of potatoes in slow cooker.
3. Add onions, peppers and garlic to skillet with 1 T. olive oil. Brown and add to slow cooker.
4. Deglaze skillet over high heat—use red wine and scrape up any brown bits. Pour in slow cooker.
5. Sprinkle ingredients with salt and pepper.
6. Pour in beef broth, tomatoes, mushrooms and barbecue sauce.
7. Cover and cook on LOW for 8 hours.
8. In a small cup, combine cold water and cornstarch until dissolved. Pour into stew and stir. Cook for one additional hour on LOW, or until stew is thickened to your preference.

Frozen peas can also be added 1 hour before stew is done.

Heartier Helpings

 # Split Pea & Sausage Soup

YIELD 10 bowls | **COOK TIME** 6 hours

Ingredients

- 1   (20-oz.) pkg. green split peas
- 1   lb. pork sausage
- 1   small onion, diced
- 1   (28-oz.) can crushed tomatoes
- ½   small head of cabbage, chopped
- 1   (32-oz.) container chicken broth
- 1   red bell pepper, chopped
- 1   t. garlic powder
-     Salt and pepper, to taste

Directions

1. Rinse and sort peas. Place in slow cooker.
2. In a large skillet over medium-high heat, cook sausage and onion together until cooked through.
3. Drain and add sausage mixture to slow cooker.
4. Add remaining ingredients and stir well.
5. Cover and cook on LOW for 6 hours.

Deliciously Lucky

This split pea and sausage soup is especially great to have on New Year's Day because it contains several ingredients that are thought to bring good luck—legumes, cabbage and pork! Serve it on the first day of the year to warm up and you just might have good fortune as well!

15-Bean Tomato and Beef Soup

YIELD 10 to 12 bowls **I COOK TIME** 8 hours

Ingredients

1 (20-oz.) pkg. 15-bean soup
1 yellow onion, chopped
2 c. diced tomatoes
2 c. mixed frozen vegetables (optional)
1 ½ lb. stewing beef
1 T. minced garlic
   Salt and pepper, to taste
1 (15-oz.) can tomato sauce
1 (64-oz.) container beef broth

Directions

1. Rinse and sort beans.
2. Place rinsed beans in slow cooker.
3. Place onion, diced tomato, frozen vegetables (if using), beef and seasonings on top of beans.
4. Pour tomato sauce evenly over ingredients.
5. Pour beef broth on top of all ingredients.
6. Cover and cook on LOW for 8 hours.
7. Remove lid, stir and let soup cool for 15 minutes before serving.

This recipe is a great-tasting source of protein!

Heartier Helpings

There's nothing like hearty vegetables to comfort the soul and nourish the body through the season!

From the Garden

A big batch of slow-cooked, steamy soups full of fresh veggies is always appreciated on a cold winter day!

Butternut Squash Soup

YIELD 5 to 6 bowls **I COOK TIME** 6 hours 30 minutes to 7 hours 30 minutes

Ingredients

- 1 (2-lb.) butternut squash, peeled, seeded and diced
- 3 leeks, sliced
- 2 tart green apples, peeled, cored and diced
- 1 T. freshly grated ginger
- 2 (14 ½-oz.) containers chicken broth
- ¾ c. water
- ¼ t. red pepper flakes
- 1 c. Parmesan cheese
- 2 c. half-and-half
- 1 t. salt, plus more to taste
- ¼ t. pepper, plus more to taste
- 5 fresh basil leaves, chopped
- ½ t. ground cinnamon

Directions

1. Combine all ingredients except cinnamon in slow cooker.
2. Cover and cook on LOW for 6 to 7 hours.
3. In small batches, puree soup using a food processor and return to slow cooker. Stir in cinnamon.
4. Cover and cook on LOW for 30 minutes.
5. Cover on WARM until ready to serve, making sure the soup does not boil.

Squash Simplified

Fresh squash tastes much better than pre-cut squash, but slicing it can be a chore. To simplify the task, slice off the bottom and top of the squash, then puncture it several times with a fork. Microwave for 3 minutes. After the squash cools slightly, peeling and slicing it should be a snap.

From the Garden

 # Cabbage Soup

YIELD 6 bowls **I COOK TIME** 8 to 10 hours

Ingredients

- 1 small head cabbage, shredded
- 1 large carrot, shredded
- 2 stalks celery, finely diced
- 1 bell pepper, finely diced
- 2 green onions, chopped
- 1 t. minced garlic
- 1 t. of Morton's Nature's Seasons Seasoning Blend
- ¼ t. red pepper flakes
- 4 c. vegetable broth
- 4 c. water
- 1 dash hot sauce

Directions

1. Add all ingredients to slow cooker.
2. Cover and cook on LOW for 8 to 10 hours.

Serve this soup with a side of sliced rye bread.

Corn and Cheese Chowder

YIELD 6 bowls **I COOK TIME** 2 to 4 hours or 6 to 9 hours

Ingredients

1	T. coconut oil
1	large yellow onion, diced
1	garlic clove, minced
2	t. ground cumin
½	t. salt
½	t. white pepper
3	c. vegetable broth
3	red potatoes, chopped
1	(14 ¾-oz.) can creamed corn
1	(12-oz.) bag frozen corn
3	slices bacon, chopped
1	c. shredded cheddar cheese
1	(12-oz.) can evaporated milk
2	T. chopped chives

Directions

1. Heat oil in a small skillet over medium. Add onion and garlic and cook until onion is translucent. Transfer mixture to slow cooker.
2. Add remaining ingredients—except cheese, evaporated milk and chives—to slow cooker. Stir well.
3. Cover and cook on LOW for 6 to 9 hours, on HIGH for 2 to 4 hours or until the potatoes are tender.
4. Add cheese and milk during the last hour of cooking. Garnish with chives and serve.

This chowder pairs perfectly with French bread and salad.

From the Garden

Creamy Asparagus Soup

YIELD 4 bowls **I COOK TIME** 3 hours 30 minutes to 4 hours 30 minutes or 7 to 8 hours

Ingredients

- 20 large spears fresh asparagus
- ½ medium white onion, chopped
- 2 small red potatoes, diced
- 3 ½ c. vegetable broth
- ½ t. seasoned salt
- ¼ t. pepper
- ½ c. half-and-half
- Salt, to taste

Directions

1. Snap ends off of asparagus, then wash and trim stems. Cut into chunks.
2. Place onion and potatoes in slow cooker, along with chopped asparagus. Add broth, seasoned salt and pepper.
3. Cover and cook on LOW for 7 to 8 hours, or on HIGH for 3 hours 30 minutes to 4 hours 30 minutes or until the potatoes are soft.
4. Using a blender, puree the soup in batches until it reaches your desired texture. Return to slow cooker and stir in half-and-half. Add salt to taste and serve when half-and-half warms.

Perfect Presentation

While you are waiting for the soup to warm back up with the half-and-half, wash and trim the other ½ lb. of asparagus, cutting off the woody ends, and steam to use as a garnish. The nice green color of the asparagus will really add an eye-catching pop to this tasty dish!

Creamy Roasted Red Pepper Soup

YIELD 4 to 6 bowls | **COOK TIME** 30 minutes

Ingredients

- 4 large tomatoes, halved and seeded
- 3 red bell peppers, halved and seeded
- 3 orange bell peppers, halved and seeded
- 1 large poblano pepper, halved and seeded
- 2 large sweet onions, quartered
- 10 leaves fresh basil, chopped
- 1–2 T. olive oil
- 1 t. salt, plus more to taste
- ¼ t. pepper, plus more to taste
- 16 slices (about 1 lb.) bacon
- 1 head roasted garlic
- 1–2 (8-oz.) packages cream cheese
  Crushed red pepper, to taste
- 1 c. Parmesan cheese
- 2 c. half-and-half

Directions

1. Place tomatoes, peppers, onions and basil in large roasting pan. Toss with olive oil, salt and pepper.
2. Stretch bacon over veggies and cook in an oven preheated to 400 degrees F, uncovered, for 30 to 45 minutes, or until veggies are brown and tender and bacon is crisp. Allow vegetables to cool, and puree with roasted garlic in a blender. Transfer mixture, along with cream cheese, into slow cooker. Add remaining ingredients.
3. Cover and cook on HIGH for 30 minutes, or until soup is hot and blended.
4. Cover on WARM until ready to serve, making sure the soup does not boil.

Chives and fresh, cracked pepper will top things off nicely.

From the Garden

Creamy Zucchini Soup

YIELD 6 bowls **I COOK TIME** 4 hours 15 minutes

Croutons add a welcome crunch to this creamy favorite!

Ingredients

- 1 small yellow onion, finely chopped
- 5 medium zucchini, chopped
- 32 oz. chicken broth
- 1 t. seasoned salt
- 1 t. dried dill weed
- ½ t. pepper
- 2 T. butter, melted
- 1 (8-oz.) container sour cream

Directions

1. Combine all ingredients (except sour cream) in slow cooker.
2. Cover and cook on LOW for 4 hours, or until zucchini is soft.
3. Carefully puree soup in slow cooker using an immersion blender.
4. Stir in sour cream until smooth. Cover and cook an additional 15 minutes.

Parmed Vegetable Soup

YIELD 10 bowls **I** **COOK TIME** 6 to 7 hours

Ingredients

- 1 lb. top sirloin, cut into cubes
- 2 bay leaves
- 3 celery stalks, washed and chopped
- 1 onion, diced
- 2 potatoes, peeled and cubed
- 4 carrots, peeled and chopped
- 2 t. garlic powder
  Salt and pepper, to taste
- 1 (28-oz.) can diced tomatoes (do not drain)
- 1 (28-oz.) container beef broth
- 1 T. olive oil
- 4 c. water
- 1 c. frozen corn
- 1 ½ c. frozen green beans
  Oyster crackers, to serve
  Parmesan or other grated cheese, to garnish

Directions

1. Place beef in slow cooker.
2. Add bay leaves, celery, onions, potatoes and carrots. Season with garlic powder, salt and pepper.
3. Pour diced tomatoes, beef broth, olive oil and water on top.
4. Cover and cook on HIGH for 5 to 6 hours.
5. Add corn and green beans.
6. Cover and cook on HIGH for 1 hour more or until vegetables are softened.
7. Serve with oyster crackers and Parmesan cheese, if desired.

Pumpkin Soup

YIELD 6 bowls **I** **COOK TIME** 6 hours 20 minutes

Ingredients

- 2 T. butter
- 1 small white onion, diced
- 1 t. minced garlic
- 2 lb. fresh roasted pumpkin flesh, cubed, or 2 (15-oz.) cans pure pumpkin puree and ½ c. water
- 2 c. chicken broth
- 2 T. fresh ginger
- 2 t. dried ginger
- 1 t. chili powder
- 1 orange, juiced
- 2 t. curry powder
- 1 (14-oz.) can coconut milk
- ¼ c. chopped fresh cilantro

Directions

1. Heat butter over medium in a large skillet. Sauté onions and garlic until onions are translucent but garlic is not burnt.
2. Transfer mixture to slow cooker. Add remaining ingredients (except coconut milk and cilantro) and stir well.
3. Cover and cook on LOW for 6 hours.
4. If using fresh pumpkin, puree soup to your preferred texture. Stir in coconut milk.
5. Cover and cook on LOW for 20 minutes.
6. Serve soup garnished with cilantro.

Tasty Ways to Top

There are many ways to serve this all-time fall-favorite soup—and they all taste great! When it comes time to serve, try topping your pumpkin soup with a sprinkle of nutmeg and a dollop of sour cream. Or, if you want some sweetness in your soup, try adding a little bit of cinnamon!

 # Roasted Cauliflower Curry Soup with Honey

YIELD 4 bowls **I COOK TIME** 6 hours

Ingredients

1	head cauliflower, cut into florets
4	T. olive oil, divided
1	t. garlic powder
1	t. salt
½	t. pepper
1	medium yellow onion, diced
2	ribs celery, chopped
1	T. yellow curry powder
2	c. chicken stock
2	c. water
2–3	dashes hot sauce
4	T. honey

This will satisfy lovers of spicy and sweet flavors alike.

Directions

1. Toss cauliflower with 2 T. olive oil, garlic powder, salt and pepper. Set aside.
2. Heat remaining 2 T. olive oil in a large skillet over medium-high. Cook onion and celery for 3 to 4 minutes. Add curry powder and continue cooking until onion is translucent.
3. In batches, cook seasoned cauliflower in the skillet just until outside is brown and soft.
4. Add onions and cauliflower to slow cooker with chicken stock, water and hot sauce.
5. Cover and cook on LOW for 6 hours.
6. Transfer batches of soup to a blender and puree until smooth. Return liquid to the slow cooker and repeat until the soup reaches desired texture. Drizzle with honey and serve.

Southwestern Potato Soup

YIELD 8 to 10 bowls **I COOK TIME** 3 hours

Ingredients

4	Yukon gold potatoes, sliced
1	t. smoked paprika
4	c. chicken stock
1	clove garlic, minced
1	c. shredded sharp cheddar cheese, plus more to garnish
1	c. corn
1	c. half-and-half
¼	c. chopped cilantro
1	(4-oz.) can diced green chilies
1	t. ground cumin
	Salt and pepper, to taste
	Bacon, to garnish

Directions

1. Place the potatoes in slow cooker. Sprinkle with paprika and add 1 c. chicken stock.
2. Cover and cook on HIGH for 2 hours, or until potatoes are tender.
3. Transfer ½ of the potatoes to a food processor or blender, along with the cooking liquid. Add garlic. Blend or process until smooth.
4. Return the mixture to slow cooker and stir in the remaining chicken stock, shredded cheese, corn, half-and-half, cilantro, green chilies, cumin, salt and pepper.
5. Cover and cook on LOW for 1 hour, or until the soup is hot.
6. Serve in individual bowls and top with cheese and bacon, if desired.

A great blend of heartiness and heat for a cozy, cold day.

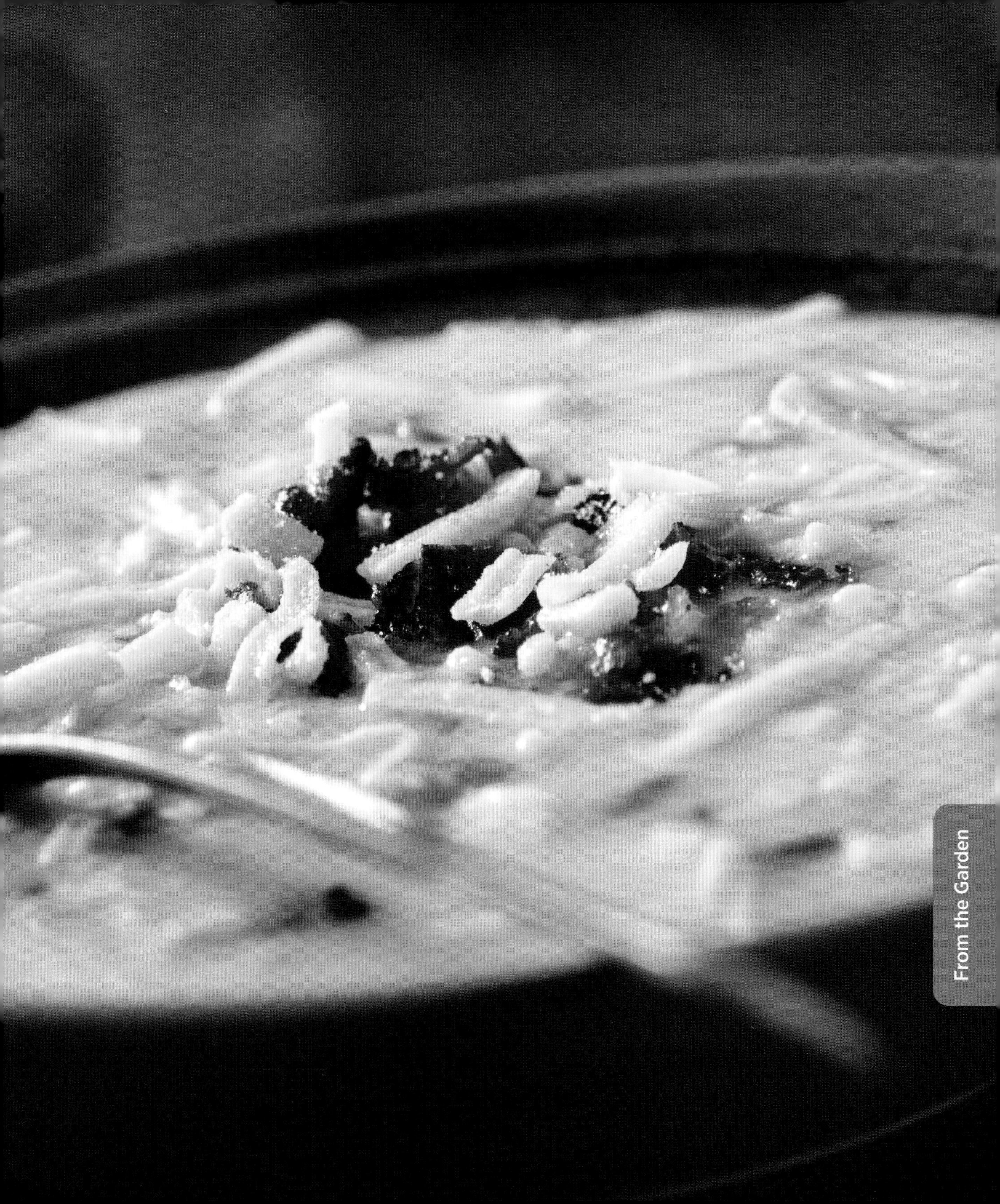

Spicy Black Bean Soup

YIELD 8 bowls **I** **COOK TIME** 3 to 4 hours

Ingredients

- 1 medium sweet onion, chopped
- 1 medium red onion, chopped
- 2 sweet bell peppers, chopped
- 1 T. olive oil
- 4 garlic cloves, minced
- 1 T. ground cumin
- 1 (16-oz.) bag black beans
- 2 T. chipotles in adobo
- 4 c. hot water
- 3 c. hot vegetable broth
- 1 lime, juiced
  Salt and pepper, to taste

Directions

1. Sauté onions and bell peppers in a skillet with olive oil over medium-high heat until slightly browned. Add garlic and cumin. Cook for 1 minute, then transfer the mixture to slow cooker.
2. Add dry beans, chipotles in adobo, water and broth.
3. Cover and cook on HIGH for 3 to 4 hours, or until beans are soft.
4. Puree ½ the slow cooker mixture in a blender until smooth. Return to slow cooker, add lime juice, salt and pepper, and stir.

Serving Suggestions

When it comes to serving this spicy black bean soup, you really can't go wrong. From all of the times I've made this dish, I've found serving it with a starch, such as steamed white rice, makes it feel like a full meal. But if you want to offer it as a starter, serve it with tortilla chips for dipping!

From the Garden

Tomato Basil Tortellini Soup

YIELD 4 to 6 bowls **I COOK TIME** 4 hours 30 minutes to 6 hours

Ingredients

- 2   T. unsalted butter
- 1   small onion, diced
- 2   t. minced garlic
- 2   (14-oz.) cans crushed tomatoes
- 1   (14.5-oz.) can diced tomatoes
- 3   T. tomato paste
- 2   T. Italian seasoning
- 1   T. sugar
     Salt and pepper, to taste
- 2   carrots, peeled and chopped
- 3   c. chicken stock
- 1   bay leaf
- ½   c. half-and-half
- 12   oz. uncooked cheese-filled tortellini
     Vegetables of your choice (optional)
     Parmesan, to garnish
     Sour cream, to garnish

Directions

1. Melt butter over low heat in a large skillet. Cook onions until translucent.
2. Stir in garlic, crushed tomatoes, diced tomatoes and tomato paste.
3. Add Italian seasonings, sugar, salt and pepper to taste.
4. Add carrots in bottom of slow cooker. Salt and pepper again, if desired.
5. Pour tomato sauce over top carrots. Pour in broth and add bay leaf.
6. Cover and cook on LOW for 4 to 5 hours.
7. Remove bay leaf and set aside.
8. Stir in half-and-half and tortellini.
9. Cover and cook on HIGH for 30 to 60 additional minutes, or until tortellini are cooked through.
10. Pour in soup bowls, sprinkle with freshly grated Parmesan cheese and serve with a dollop of sour cream.

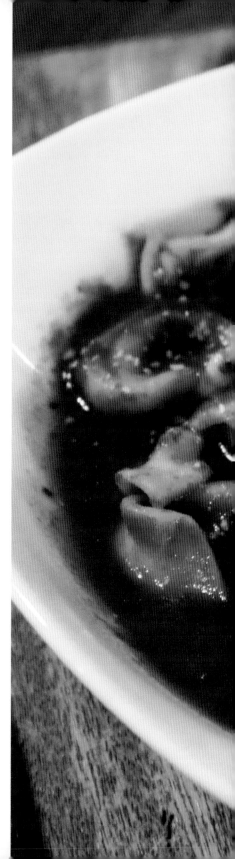

 # Vegetable Noodle Soup

YIELD 6 to 8 bowls **I COOK TIME** 2 hours 30 minutes to 3 hours 30 minutes
or 6 hours 30 minutes to 8 hours 30 minutes

Ingredients

- 2 medium yellow onions, chopped
- 3 large carrots, peeled and sliced
- 2 stalks celery, sliced
- 2 c. diced broccoli florets
- 1 t. salt
- ¼ t. pepper
- 4 c. chicken broth
- 1 (6-oz.) package pasta
- 3 T. fresh parsley, chopped
- 2 T. lemon juice

Directions

1. Mix all ingredients (except pasta, parsley and lemon juice) in slow cooker.
2. Cover and cook on LOW for 6 to 8 hours or on HIGH for 2 to 3 hours.
3. Stir in noodles, parsley and lemon juice.
4. Cover and cook on HIGH for 30 minutes.

Vegetable and Barley Soup

Feel free to add more tomatoes for more flavor!

YIELD 8 bowls **I COOK TIME** 6 hours 15 minutes to 8 hours 15 minutes

Ingredients

- 2 medium yellow onions, diced
- 2 carrots, peeled and sliced
- 2 celery stalks, thinly sliced
- 3 c. water
- 1 c. tomato juice
- 4 c. vegetable broth or stock
- 1 t. salt
- 1 t. basil
- ½ t. thyme
- ½ t. pepper
- ½ t. celery salt
- 1 c. pearl barley
- 2 c. green beans
- 2 T. dill
- 2 red potatoes, washed and chopped into ¾-in. pieces
- 1 (14 ½-oz.) can diced fire roasted tomatoes, undrained

Directions

1. Place all ingredients (except tomatoes) in slow cooker.
2. Cover and cook on LOW for 6 to 8 hours.
3. Stir soup and add tomatoes.
4. Cover and cook on LOW for 15 minutes.

From the Garden

Vegetarian Minestrone

YIELD 12 bowls **I COOK TIME** 6 hours 30 minutes

Ingredients

- 6 c. vegetable broth
- 1 (28-oz.) can crushed tomatoes
- 1 (15-oz.) can kidney beans, drained
- 1 large yellow onion, chopped
- 2 stalks celery, chopped
- 2 large carrots, chopped
- 1 ½ c. green beans
- 1 small zucchini, chopped
- 2 cloves garlic, minced
- 1 T. parsley
- 1 ½ t. dried oregano
- ¾ t. sage
- ¾ t. dried thyme
- 2 bay leaves
- ¼ t. pepper
- 1 t. salt
- 5 fresh basil leaves, chopped
- ½ c. uncooked pasta
- 4 c. fresh spinach, chopped
- 1 ¼ c. fresh and finely grated Parmesan cheese
- 2 c. half-and-half

Directions

1. Combine ingredients (except pasta, spinach, cheese and half-and-half) in slow cooker.
2. Cover and cook on LOW for 6 hours.
3. Stir in pasta, spinach, 1 c. Parmesan and half-and-half.
4. Cover and cook on HIGH for 30 minutes.
5. Remove bay leaves, top with remaining cheese and serve.
6. Cover on WARM until ready to serve, making sure the soup does not boil.

From the Garden

Vegetarian
Red Bean Soup

YIELD 12 bowls **I COOK TIME** 6 hours

Ingredients

- 3   stalks celery, chopped
- 2   medium yellow onions, chopped
- 2   t. minced garlic
- 2   (14 ½-oz.) cans diced tomatoes
- 1   (8-oz.) can corn
- 4   (16-oz.) cans red kidney beans, rinsed and drained
- 4   c. vegetable broth
- 2   bay leaves
- 1   t. salt
- 1   t. Cajun seasoning
- ½   t. pepper
- ½   t. red pepper flakes
- ½   t. allspice
- 1   c. sour cream, for garnish

Directions

1. Place celery and onions in the bottom of slow cooker. Stir in remaining ingredients (except sour cream).
2. Cover and cook on LOW for 6 hours, or until veggies are tender.
3. Discard bay leaves, serve in individual bowls and top with sour cream, if desired.

Parsley will add a nice green to this red-heavy soup.

Cheesy Cauliflower Soup

YIELD 6 bowls **I COOK TIME** 4 to 6 hours

Ingredients

- 2 heads fresh cauliflower, chopped
- 1 medium onion, chopped
- 1 celery rib, chopped
- 1 T. dried dill
- 4 c. chicken broth or vegetable broth
- 2 c. half-and-half
- ½ t. Worcestershire sauce
- 1 c. cheddar cheese, grated
- ¼ t. salt
- ⅛ t. pepper

Directions

1. Combine cauliflower, onion, celery, dill and broth in slow cooker.
2. Cover and cook on LOW for 4 to 6 hours.
3. In small batches, puree in blender or use a stick blender.
4. Transfer back to slow cooker and blend in half-and-half, Worcestershire sauce and cheese.
5. Add salt and pepper to taste.

Top off with a little extra cheese and serve this savory soup in a mug.

From the Garden

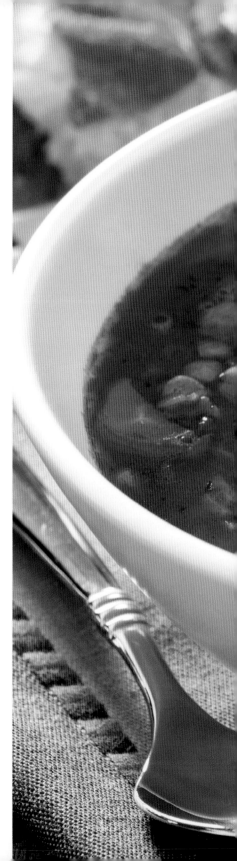

Greek Lentil Soup

YIELD 8 bowls **| COOK TIME** 6 hours 30 minutes to 8 hours 30 minutes

Ingredients

- 1 ½ c. dried lentils
- 1 (32-oz.) container beef broth
- 1 medium yellow onion, chopped
- 1 carrot, peeled and chopped
- 1 stalk celery, chopped
- 1 t. salt
- ⅛ t. pepper
- 3 T. olive oil
- 1 bay leaf
- 2 cloves garlic, minced
- ½ t. dried oregano
- 1 (14.5-oz.) can diced tomatoes
- 3 T. red wine vinegar

Directions

1. Place lentils and beef stock in slow cooker.
2. Sauté onion, carrot, celery and salt and pepper in oil in a large skillet at medium heat until onion is translucent. Add to slow cooker.
3. Add bay leaf, garlic, salt and oregano to slow cooker.
4. Cover and cook on LOW for 6 to 8 hours.
5. Add diced tomatoes and vinegar. Stir well.
6. Cover and cook on HIGH for 30 minutes. Remove bay leaf and serve.

Change It Up

Making little changes to a recipe is a great way to bring a fresh taste to an old favorite, and this soup is perfect for that. To add a little more zip to your Greek lentil soup, in step 3, increase oregano to 1 t. and add ½–1 t. of ground cumin. If your family likes bold flavors, they'll be glad you did!

 Apple and Parsnip Soup

YIELD 8 bowls **I COOK TIME** 10 to 12 hours

Ingredients

- 6 parsnips, peeled and cut into 2-in. pieces
- 2 large red apples, peeled, cored and quartered
- 1 large yellow onion, finely chopped
- 1 (32-oz.) container vegetable broth
- 1 c. water
- 2 sprigs fresh thyme
- 1 t. freshly grated ginger
- ½ t. salt
- 2 cloves garlic, minced
  Olive oil, to garnish

Directions

1. Place all ingredients (except olive oil) in slow cooker. Stir.
2. Cover and cook on LOW for 10 to 12 hours, or until vegetables are tender.
3. Turn off slow cooker, uncover and remove thyme sprigs.
4. Transfer soup to a blender in small batches and puree until smooth. Return to slow cooker.
5. Garnish with olive oil and serve immediately.

You can swap the vegetable broth for chicken broth.

From the Garden

 # Squash and Apple Bisque

YIELD 8 bowls **I** **COOK TIME** 3 to 5 hours or 8 to 10 hours

Ingredients

2	lb. butternut squash, peeled and cubed
1	small yellow onion, chopped
1	(14 ½-oz.) container chicken broth
3	c. peeled, sliced apples
1	t. ground ginger
¼	t. salt
½	c. sour cream

Directions

1. Mix all ingredients except sour cream in slow cooker.
2. Cover and cook on LOW for 8 to 10 hours or on HIGH for 3 to 5 hours, or until squash is tender.
3. Use an immersion (stick) blender to blend ingredients and thicken soup.
4. Stir in sour cream.
5. Cover and cook on LOW for 15 to 20 minutes or until soup is fully heated.
6. Garnish each serving with a dollop of sour cream.

Paleo
Pumpkin and Kale Stew

YIELD 8 bowls **I COOK TIME** 3 hours 30 minutes

Ingredients

- ¼ c. olive oil
- 1 c. yellow onion
- 1 t. sea salt
- 1 ¼ t. ground ginger
- 1 cinnamon stick
- ¼ t. ground cumin
- ⅛ t. cayenne pepper
  Freshly ground black pepper
- 1 lb. fingerling potatoes
- 1 lb. carrots
- 3 turnips, peeled and chopped
- 3 c. chicken or vegetable broth
- 2 lb. sugar baby pumpkin, peeled, seeded and diced
- 1 lb. sweet potatoes, peeled and diced into large pieces
- ½ c. golden raisins
- 1 T. raw honey
- 4 c. loosely packed kale
- 1–2 T. apple cider vinegar

Using vegetable broth makes this stew vegan-friendly!

Directions

1. Heat oil over medium-high in large skillet; add onions and salt and sauté until soft, about 4 minutes. Add ginger, cinnamon, cumin, cayenne and a pinch of pepper and for cook about 1 minute.
2. Place seasoned onions in slow cooker.
3. Combine potatoes, carrots, turnips and broth with onions and stir.
4. Cover and cook on HIGH for 1 hour and 30 minutes.
5. Add pumpkin, sweet potatoes, raisins, honey and a bit more salt to taste, if desired. Stir.
6. Re-cover and continue to cook on HIGH for about 2 more hours, or until vegetables are quite soft.
7. Add kale and gently stir. Let kale wilt then add apple cider vinegar to taste.
8. Season with more salt and pepper, if desired.

From the Garden

Tortellini Squash Stew

YIELD 6 bowls **I** **COOK TIME** 6 hours 20 minutes to 7 hours 25 minutes

Ingredients

2	T. olive oil
1	large onion, diced
¾	t. salt
2	lb. butternut squash, peeled and cubed or 16 oz. frozen diced butternut squash
1	large zucchini, cut in 1-in. chunks
1	large yellow summer squash, cut in 1-in. chunks
1	large red bell pepper, cut in ½-in. dice
2	(14-oz.) cans crushed tomatoes
1	(14 ½-oz.) container broth, chicken or vegetable
1	T. dried oregano, chopped
⅛	t. freshly ground black pepper
9	oz. fresh cheese tortellini
5	oz. baby spinach
3	T. Parmesan cheese, grated

Directions

1. Heat oil in a large skillet over medium-high heat; add onion and salt and sauté until transluscent. Transfer to slow cooker.
2. Top onions with butternut squash, zucchini, yellow summer squash, bell pepper, tomatoes, broth, oregano and salt and pepper.
3. Cover and cook on LOW for 6 to 7 hours.
4. Remove lid and lightly mash vegetables. Stir in tortellini.
5. Cover and cook for 15 to 20 minutes until pasta is al dante. Add spinach and Parmesan, gently stir.
6. Cover and cook for about 5 minutes or until spinach is wilted.

Fresh breadsticks make delicious dippers for this stew!

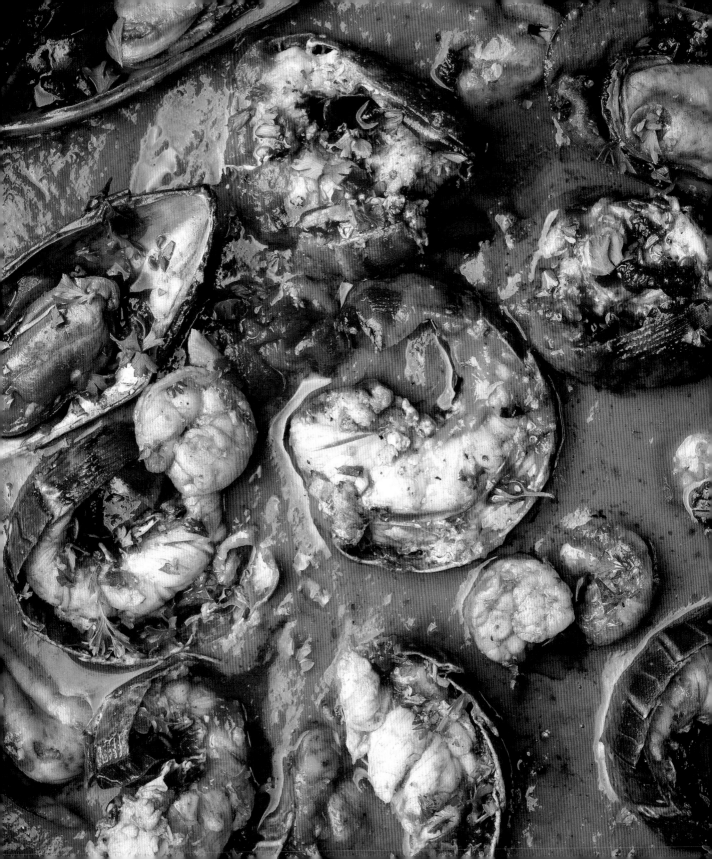

Get ready to serve up the seafood you and your family crave!

From the Sea

All it takes is one taste, and these seafood favorites will be reeling your family in to the dinner table night after night!

Fisherman's Cioppino Stew

YIELD 6 bowls **I** **COOK TIME** 6 to 8 hours

Ingredients

- 2 (14-oz.) cans crushed tomatoes
- 1 (8-oz.) can tomato sauce
- ½ c. chopped onion
- 1 c. wine, white and dry
- ⅓ c. olive oil
- 3 garlic cloves, minced
- ½ c. parsley, chopped
- 1 green pepper, chopped
- 1 hot pepper, chopped (optional)
- Salt and pepper, to taste
- 1 t. thyme
- 2 t. basil
- 1 t. oregano
- ½ t. paprika
- ½ t. cayenne pepper

SEAFOOD

- 1 fillet of seabass, cod or other whitefish, deboned and cubed
- 12 prawns
- 12 scallops
- 12 mussels
- 12 clams (can use canned)

Directions

1. Place all ingredients in slow cooker except seafood.
2. Cover and cook on LOW for 6 to 8 hours.
3. About 30 minutes before serving, add selected seafood.
4. Turn up slow cooker to HIGH and gently stir occasionally.

Add a little lemon juice just before serving.

Chicken Clam Chowder

YIELD 10 to 12 bowls **| COOK TIME** 4 hours 30 minutes or 6 hours 30 minutes to 7 hours 30 minutes

Ingredients

16	slices bacon, diced
2	medium yellow onions, chopped
4	stalks celery, diced
½	t. salt
½	t. pepper
3	large potatoes, peeled and diced
2	boneless, skinless chicken breasts
4	c. chicken broth
2	(8-oz.) bottles clam juice
1	(15-oz.) can sweet corn
¾	c. flour
4	c. milk
4	c. shredded white cheddar cheese
½	c. heavy whipping cream
2	T. parsley

Directions

1. Sauté bacon, onions and celery in skillet until bacon is crisp and onions are translucent. Add salt and pepper to mixture.
2. Place the potatoes, chicken, chicken broth, clam juice and corn in slow cooker. Pour skillet mixture over top.
3. Cover and cook on LOW for 6 to 7 hours or on HIGH for 4 hours.
4. Remove chicken and cut into ½-in. pieces. Return meat to slow cooker and set to HIGH.
5. In a small bowl, whisk flour into milk. Stir into soup, along with cheese, whipping cream and parsley.
6. Cover and cook on HIGH for 30 minutes.

This chowder can serve as a complete meal on its own.

 # Crab and Corn Soup

YIELD 8 bowls **I** **COOK TIME** 8 hours

Ingredients

2	T. butter
1	medium yellow onion, diced
1	sweet bell pepper, diced
4	c. chicken broth
1	parsnip, diced
⅓	t. thyme
1	(4-oz.) jar green chilies, drained
1	c. frozen corn
2	(6-oz.) cans crabmeat
½	t. chili powder
1	dash salt
1	dash pepper
2	large carrots, slivered
1	c. coconut milk

Directions

1. Heat butter in skillet over medium. Once butter has melted, sauté onions until they are translucent, then transfer them to slow cooker. Add remaining ingredients (except coconut milk).
2. Cover and cook on LOW for 8 hours.
3. Add coconut milk, stir well and turn off slow cooker. Serve immediately in bowls.

If you're not keen on corn, zucchini works well, too.

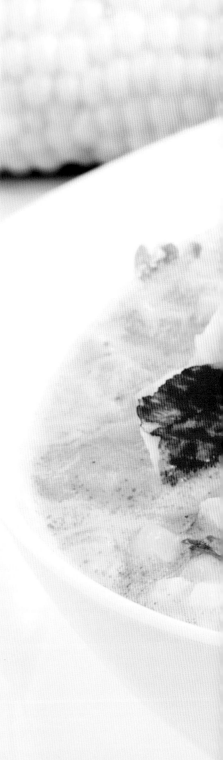

Easy
Cream of Crab Soup

YIELD 4 to 6 bowls **I** **COOK TIME** 3 to 6 hours

Ingredients

- 1   (16-oz.) can lump crabmeat
- 2   c. milk
- 2   c. half-and-half
- 3   T. unsalted butter
- ½   lemon, zested
- ½   small yellow onion, diced
- 1   dash paprika
- ½   t. ground nutmeg
- ½   t. salt
- ½   t. pepper
- 2   T. sherry

Directions

1. Combine all ingredients (except sherry) in slow cooker. Stir well.
2. Cover and cook on LOW for 3 to 4 hours.
3. Before serving, stir in sherry.

Best with Bread

This cream of crab soup really goes to a new level of deliciousness when you serve it with fresh-baked bread. You can either bake it yourself or buy a fresh loaf from the store (I recommend sourdough or French bread). Once it's toasty, break it up and serve it on the side or right in the bowl!

Fish Chowder

YIELD 10 to 12 bowls **I** **COOK TIME** 10 hours 30 minutes

Ingredients

- 3 lb. white fish, any variety, cut into small pieces
- 2 (32-oz.) containers chicken broth
- 10 small red potatoes, chopped
- 1 medium butternut squash, peeled, seeded and chopped
- 1 medium yellow onion, chopped
- 3 large carrots, peeled and chopped
- 4 garlic cloves, minced
- ½ T. Chinese 5-spice
- 8 slices bacon, cooked and crumbled
- 2 (10- to 12-oz.) cans full-fat coconut milk
  Salt and pepper, to taste

Directions

1. Add fish, chicken broth, vegetables, garlic, Chinese 5-spice and bacon to slow cooker. Stir to combine.
2. Cover and cook on LOW for 10 hours.
3. Transfer ½ the soup to a blender and puree. Return soup to the slow cooker. Add coconut milk, salt and pepper.
4. Cover and cook on LOW for 30 minutes.

Chunky Chowder

If you want your chowder to be extra hearty, you can choose to puree only a small portion of the batch, leaving more fish and veggie chunks intact. Another option is to cook the fish separately and stir into the mostly pureed soup just a few minutes before serving time.

Lobster Bisque

YIELD 7 to 8 bowls | **COOK TIME** 3 hours 20 minutes to 6 hours 20 minutes

Ingredients

- 2   T. butter
- 2   shallots, finely minced
- 1   garlic clove, finely minced
- 1   (32-oz.) container seafood stock
- 2   t. tarragon
- 2   t. thyme
- ½   t. pepper
- ¾   t. paprika
- ¼   c. parsley
- 1   (14 ½-oz.) can diced tomatoes
- 1   (6-oz.) can tomato paste
- ½   c. water
- 4   lobster tails, halved and meat removed
- 2   c. heavy cream
- ¼–½ c. sherry, to garnish

Serve on the side of a steak dinner for an easy "surf and turf" meal.

Directions

1. Heat butter in a skillet over medium. When butter melts, sauté shallots. Add garlic and cook for 1 to 2 minutes. If garlic burns, discard and repeat step. Transfer skillet mixture to slow cooker.
2. Add seafood stock, tarragon, thyme, pepper, paprika, parsley, tomatoes, tomato paste and water and stir.
3. Cover and cook on LOW for 6 hours or on HIGH for 3 hours.
4. Blend the soup in small batches until it reaches desired texture. Cover slow cooker and set to HIGH.
5. Remove any veiny pieces from the lobster meat. Chop into small chunks and transfer to the slow cooker.
6. Cover and cook on HIGH for 20 minutes, or until meat is cooked through.
7. Stir in heavy cream. Serve in individual bowls and top each portion with sherry.

From the Sea

Seafood Bacon Chowder

YIELD 4 bowls **I** **COOK TIME** 5 hours 30 minutes
to 5 hours 45 minutes

Ingredients

- 4 slices bacon, diced
- 2-3 medium potatoes, diced
- 1 medium yellow onion, diced
- ½ lb. white fish, any variety, cut into chunks
- 2 c. milk
- 1 c. plus 2 T. water, divided
- 1 bay leaf
- 1 T. Worcestershire sauce
- 1 T. cornstarch
- ½ c. shrimp or scallops

Directions

1. Heat bacon in a skillet over medium-high until fat runs. Drain fat, add potatoes and onions and cook for 5 minutes, or until potatoes begin to soften.
2. Transfer skillet mixture to slow cooker and add white fish. Stir lightly. Add milk, 1 c. water, bay leaf and Worcestershire sauce.
3. Cover and cook on LOW for 5 hours.
4. In a small bowl, combine cornstarch and remaining 2 T. water until smooth. Pour the mixture into the chowder to thicken. Stir well. Add shrimp or scallops and stir.
5. Cover and cook on HIGH for 30 to 45 minutes.

Serve with a tossed salad and you have a complete meal!

 Potato Crab Chowder

YIELD 6 to 8 bowls **I COOK TIME** 4 to 5 hours

Ingredients

4	small red potatoes, cleaned and quartered
¾	c. chopped carrots
1	medium yellow onion, chopped
1	t. dried thyme
1	t. garlic, minced
¼	t. black pepper
3	c. chicken broth
½	c. water
1	c. evaporated milk
3	T. cornstarch
10	oz. frozen corn
1	(6-oz.) can crabmeat, drained
½	c. sliced green onions

Directions

1. Place potatoes and carrots in the bottom of slow cooker. Add onion on top of potatoes/carrots.
2. Add thyme, garlic and pepper.
3. Pour broth and water into slow cooker.
4. Cover and cook on LOW for 3 to 4 hours.
5. After 3 to 4 hours, stir together evaporated milk and cornstarch in a medium bowl until smooth.
6. Pour milk mixture into slow cooker and stir ingredients. Lightly mash potatoes, then stir in corn.
7. Re-cover and cook on LOW for 1 hour.
8. Stir in crabmeat and green onions right before serving.

Crumble crackers on top for a little bit of crunch.

Creamy Shrimp Bisque

YIELD 4 bowls **|** COOK TIME 3 to 4 hours

Ingredients

- 2 T. butter
- 1 c. sliced mushrooms
- 2 T. sliced green onion
- 1 garlic clove, minced
- 1 (14-oz.) container chicken broth
- ¼ c. tomato paste
- 3 T. all-purpose flour
- ½ c. light cream
- ½ c. dry white wine
- 1 lb. frozen shrimp, shelled and deveined
- 1 T. chopped fresh parsley

Directions

1. In a large skillet, melt butter and add mushrooms, green onion and garlic until translucent, stirring occasionally.
2. Add broth and tomato paste.
3. In a separate bowl, stir together the flour and cream until well blended and smooth. Stir into broth mixture.
4. Transfer to slow cooker. Cover and cook on LOW for 3 to 4 hours.
5. If bisque is thin, add cornstarch or flour to cold water and make sure all lumps are out.
6. About 30 minutes before bisque is done, add wine and shrimp and stir into bisque.
7. Cover and continue to cook for the last 30 minutes.
8. Sprinkle parsley on bisque in serving bowls.

Fish Congee

YIELD 6 bowls **I** **COOK TIME** 5 to 6 hours or 8 to 12 hours

Ingredients

- 1 lb. cod fish, cut into large chunks
- 1 T. fish sauce
- 1 T. soy sauce
- 1 T. sesame oil
- ½ t. white pepper
- 1 c. jasmine rice
- 8 c. water
- 1 (1-in.) piece ginger, grated
- 2 green onions, sliced
- Salt, to taste
- Fried onion pieces, to garnish
- Fried garlic bits, to garnish

Directions

1. In a bowl, marinate fish in fish sauce, soy sauce, sesame oil and white pepper. Put in refrigerator until ready to use.
2. Place rice, water, ginger, onions and salt in slow cooker. Stir to combine then add marinated fish.
3. Cover and cook on HIGH for 5 to 6 hours or on LOW for 8 to 12 hours. Serve with fried onion pieces or fried garlic bits.

Change It Up

Fish congee is a type of porridge commonly eaten in many Asian countries. You can use any type of fish you prefer when you make it! I like haddock best, but I've also found other fish like cod and salmon are great in it, too.

From the Sea

 # Salmon Chowder

YIELD 4 bowls **I** COOK TIME 4 hours 30 minutes

Ingredients

- ½ yellow onion, chopped
- 3 celery stalks, washed and chopped
- 4 oz. shredded carrots
- 4 c. chicken broth
- 5 oz. frozen corn
- 5 oz. frozen peas
- ½ c. rice
- 1 t. minced garlic
- 1 t. dried dill
- 1 t. smoked paprika
- 12 oz. Alaskan salmon, drained and flaked
- 1 (8-oz.) pkg. cream cheese, softened

Directions

1. Combine all ingredients except salmon and cream cheese in slow cooker.
2. Cover and cook on LOW for 4 hours.
3. Add cream cheese and salmon to slow cooker. Stir to combine.
4. Cover and cook for an additional 30 minutes or until cream cheese is fully melted. Stir well to combine and serve.

Big chunks of salmon will make every spoonful satisfying.

Slow Cooker Jambalaya

YIELD 5 to 6 bowls **I COOK TIME** 4 hours 15 minutes

Ingredients

- 1 Rotisserie chicken, cut into 1 ½-in. pieces
- 1 medium red onion, diced
- 1 large white onion, diced
- 1 large carrot, peeled and sliced
- 1 T. minced garlic
- 1 t. hot sauce
- 2 T. tomato paste
- 1 t. cumin
- 1 t. basil
- 1 t. coarse salt
- ½ t. pepper
- 1 (14-oz.) can diced tomatoes
- 1 lb. raw shrimp, peeled and deveined
- 2 c. cooked rice, optional

Directions

1. Combine all ingredients except shrimp and rice in slow cooker.
2. Cover and cook on LOW for 4 hours.
3. Add shrimp and stir.
4. Cover and cook on HIGH for an additional 15 minutes.
5. Serve over hot, freshly cooked rice.

Get creative with your own garnishes and extra seasonings.

 # Oyster Soup

YIELD 8 to 10 bowls **I COOK TIME** 4 to 5 hours

Ingredients

- 6 c. milk
- 2 T. flour mixed with 2 T. water
- 4 T. butter
  Salt and white pepper, to taste
- 1 t. Worcestershire sauce
- 1 t. cayenne pepper
- 2 (8-oz.) cans of whole oysters (with liquid)

Directions

1. Put all ingredients except oysters in slow cooker and stir.
2. Cover and cook on HIGH for 2 hours.
3. Stir oysters in with ingredients in slow cooker.
4. Cover and cook on LOW for 2 to 3 hours.

Seafood and Citrus

If you're a fan of seafood, you probably know that a little lemon juice adds a lot of flavor to fish. Because oysters are slightly different from other commonly eaten fish, I find this soup is best served with a lemon wedge right in it. Simply slice a wedge and add it to the bowl when serving.

New England Clam Chowder

YIELD 8 bowls | COOK TIME 3 to 4 hours

Ingredients

4–6 (6 ½-oz.) cans minced clams, juice reserved

½ lb. diced bacon

1 medium yellow onion, minced

1 celery stalk, chopped

1 t. minced garlic

6 medium russet potatoes, peeled, and cut into 1-in. cubes

1 c. water

2 t. salt

¼ t. white pepper

4 c. half-and-half

3 T. cornstarch

Chopped fresh parsley, for garnish

Oyster crackers will make this classic even better.

Directions

1. Drain clams and reserve juice. Cover clams and refrigerate.

2. Cook bacon in a large skillet over medium-high heat. Spoon most of the grease from the skillet.

3. After one minute, add onions. Cook for 3 minutes and then add reserved juice from clams.

4. Cook for 5 minutes over medium-high heat.

5. Pour bacon, onions and clam juice into slow cooker.

6. Add all remaining ingredients except clams, half-and-half, cornstarch and parsley.

7. Cover and cook on HIGH for 4 hours or until vegetables are tender.

8. Stir cornstarch into half-and-half and add to slow cooker.

9. Stir in clams.

10. Cover and cook for 1 additional hour on LOW.

11. Garnish with parsley and serve with warm bread or in a bread bowl.

From the Sea

Bayside Bouillabaisse

YIELD 8 bowls **I COOK TIME** 4 hours 10 minutes

Ingredients

- 2 T. olive oil
- 1 large white onion, diced
- 2 garlic cloves, minced
- 2 medium tomatoes, diced
- 1 large fennel bulb, diced and fronds chopped
- 3 medium klondike potatoes, cut into small cubes
- 1 t. salt
- ½ t. pepper
- 1 pinch saffron
- 1 bay leaf
- 9 c. fish stock
- 1 lb. firm white fish, any variety
- 1 lb. large shrimp, deveined and uncooked
- 12 mussels

Directions

1. Heat olive oil in a pot over medium. Add onions and garlic and sauté until onion is translucent. Stir in the tomatoes and fennel fronds. Cook for 2 to 3 minutes.
2. Add potatoes, fennel bulb, salt and pepper to slow cooker. Transfer onion mixture to the slow cooker. Add saffron, bay leaf and fish stock.
3. Cover and cook on HIGH for 4 hours, or until potatoes are tender.
4. Add white fish, shrimp and mussels and replace lid.
5. Cook on HIGH for 10 minutes, or until fish is cooked through and mussels are open wide.
6. Remove bay leaf and any mussels that did not open and serve immediately.

Removing closed mussels is essential as they may not have cooked all the way.

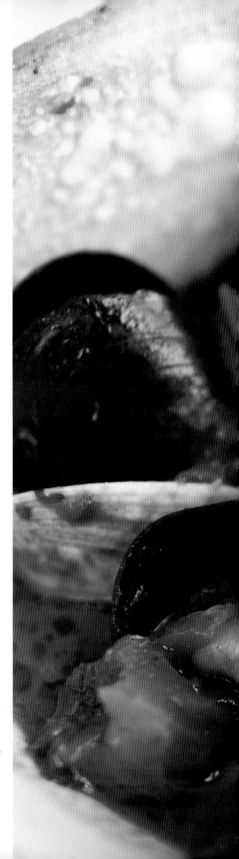

 Simple
Shrimp Pho

YIELD 4 to 5 bowls **I** **COOK TIME** 6 hours 15 minutes

Ingredients

- 8 oz. mushrooms, chopped
- 1 T. lemon zest
- 1 lime, juiced
- 2 t. fish sauce
- 2 garlic cloves, minced
- 2 T. chopped green onion
- 1 T. chopped fresh jalapeño
- 1 t. ground ginger
- 2 t. sesame oil
- 3 T. chopped fresh cilantro, plus more for garnish
- 6 c. chicken or vegetable broth
- 1 lb. shrimp, peeled and deveined

Cooked rice noodles

Directions

1. Place all ingredients except shrimp and noodles in slow cooker.
2. Cover and cook on LOW for 6 hours.
3. Stir in shrimp.
4. Cover and cook for 15 minutes or just until shrimp is done.
5. Place prepared noodles in bowls and top with soup. Garnish with additional cilantro when serving.

Pick your Kick

When it comes to spicy foods, everyone has different preferences for just how hot they like it—especially in my house! This simple shrimp pho can easily cater to all preferences if you just leave out the jalapeños. Instead of stirring them in, sauté the jalapeños and serve them on the side!

From the Sea

Conversion Guide

Volume

¼ teaspoon = 1 mL

½ teaspoon = 2 mL

1 teaspoon = 5 mL

1 tablespoon = 15 mL

¼ cup = 50mL

⅓ cup = 75 mL

½ cup = 125 mL

⅔ cup = 150 mL

¾ cup = 175 mL

1 cup = 250 mL

1 quart = 1 liter

Weight

1 ounce = 30 grams

2 ounces = 55 grams

3 ounces = 85 grams

4 ounces (¼ pound) = 115 grams

8 ounces (½ pound) = 225 grams

16 ounces (1 pound) = 455 grams

2 pounds = 910 grams

Temperatures

32° Fahrenheit = 0° Celsius

212°F = 100°C

250°F = 120°C

275°F =140°C

300°F = 150°C

325°F = 160°C

350°F = 180°C

375°F = 190°C

400°F = 200°C

425°F = 220°C

450°F = 230°C

475°F = 240°C

500°F = 260°C

Length

⅛ inch = 3 mm

¼ inch = 6 mm

½ inch = 13 mm

¾ inch = 19 mm

1 inch = 2 ½ cm

2 inches = 5 cm

Media Lab Books
For inquiries, call 646-838-6637

Copyright 2016 Topix Media Lab

Published by Topix Media Lab
14 Wall Street, Suite 4B
New York, NY 10005

Printed in China

ISBN-10: 1-942556-54-3
ISBN-13: 978-1-942556-54-1

--

CEO Tony Romando

Vice President of Brand Marketing Joy Bomba
Director of Finance Vandana Patel
Director of Sales and New Markets Tom Mifsud
Manufacturing Director Nancy Puskuldjian
Financial Analyst Matthew Quinn
Brand Marketing Assistant Taylor Hamilton

Editor-in-Chief Jeff Ashworth
Creative Director Steven Charny
Photo Director Dave Weiss
Managing Editor Courtney Kerrigan
Senior Editors Tim Baker, James Ellis

Content Editor Trevor Courneen
Content Designer Michelle Lock
Content Photo Editor Meg Reinhardt
Art Director Susan Dazzo
Assistant Managing Editor Holland Baker
Designer Danielle Santucci
Assistant Editors Alicia Kort, Kaytie Norman
Editorial Assistant Isabella Torchia

Co-Founders Bob Lee, Tony Romando

Indexing by R studio T, NYC

Special Thanks: Marsha Bare, Rachel Garmers, Jessica Pethtel

Cover Photography by Cultura/Brett Stevens/Plainpicture
Back Cover Photography by Shutterstock

Interior Photography by Jenn Bare, Shutterstock, Fotolia, and iStock
Interior Illustrations by Nikita Tcherednikov/The Noun Project; Julia Söderberg/The Noun Project; Hea Poh Lin/The Noun Project; Artem
Kovyazin/The Noun Project; Nut Chanut/The Noun Project; Pavel Melnikov/The Noun Project; Yu luck/The Noun Project; icon 54/The Noun
Project; Anbileru Adaleru/The Noun Project; Ludmil/The Noun Project; Artem Kovyazin/The Noun Project; Cédric Villain/The Noun Project;
Michael Wohlwend/The Noun Project; yugudesign.com/The Noun Project; Oliviu Stoian/The Noun Project; Vectors Market/The Noun Project; To
Uyen/The Noun Project; Amos Meron/The Noun Project; Creative Stall/The Noun Project; Muharrem Fevzi Çelik/The Noun Project; Julian Roman/
The Noun Project; Yi Chen/The Noun Project; Marco Galtarossa/The Noun Project; Verena Gutentag/The Noun Project; Gregory Sujkowski/The
Noun Project; Rachel Dangerfield/The Noun Project; Ealancheliyan s/The Noun Project; Claire Jones/The Noun Project; Unrecognized MJ/The
Noun Project; Okan Benn/The Noun Project; Edward Boatman/The Noun Project

Index

Dad's Famous No-Bean Chili 68